The Global Village Revisited

The Global Village Revisited

Art, Politics, and Television Talk Shows

Kathleen Dixon

LEXINGTON BOOKS
A division of
ROWMAN & LITTLEFIELD PUBLISHERS, INC.
Lanham • Boulder • New York • Toronto • Plymouth, UK

Published by Lexington Books
A division of Rowman & Littlefield Publishers, Inc.
A wholly owned subsidiary of The Rowman & Littlefield Publishing Group, Inc.
4501 Forbes Boulevard, Suite 200, Lanham, Maryland 20706
http://www.lexingtonbooks.com

Estover Road, Plymouth PL6 7PY, United Kingdom

Copyright © 2009 by Lexington Books

British Library Cataloguing in Publication Information Available

Library of Congress Cataloging-in-Publication Data

Dixon, Kathleen, 1955–
   The global village revisited : art, politics, and television talk shows / Kathleen Dixon.
      p. cm.
   Includes index.
   ISBN 978-0-7391-2340-9 (cloth : alk. paper) — ISBN 978-0-7391-4078-9 (electronic)
   1. Television talk shows. 2. Television—Social aspects. 3. Television and politics. 4.
Television broadcasting—Influence. l. Title.
   PN1992.8.T3D59 2009
   791.45'6—dc22   2009018345

∞ ™ The paper used in this publication meets the minimum requirements of
American National Standard for Information Sciences—Permanence of Paper for
Printed Library Materials, ANSI/NISO Z39.48-1992.

Printed in the United States of America

To philosopher-teachers everywhere, but especially Joan Graham, who led me to Ann Berthoff, and Jay Robinson, who introduced me to the work of M. M. Bakhtin.

~

Contents

	Acknowledgments	ix
Chapter 1	Introduction	1
Chapter 2	*Jan Publiek* of Belgium: Flemish Finale	27
Chapter 3	*Showto Na Slavi* of Bulgaria: Vox Populi *Kathleen Dixon and Iskra Velinova*	63
Chapter 4	The *Oprah Winfrey Show* of the United States: Melodramatic Citizen *Kathleen Dixon and Kacie Jossart*	85
Chapter 5	Conclusion	109
	Works Cited	119
	Index	127

~

Acknowledgments

The University of North Dakota (UND) funded several research awards during the period of 2001–2006 that made it possible to travel abroad and to hire translators and research assistants. The Bulgarian-American Fulbright Association funded a semester of study in the Cultural Studies Department at Sofia University in 2007. I owe a special debt to Deputy Dean Daniela Koleva, who first extended the invitation to Sofia University, and to Julia Stefanova, the director of the Bulgarian-Fulbright Association. Sofia University also offered a course in beginning Bulgarian, a definite aid to the research. Professor Alexander Kiossev, head of the cultural studies department, graciously gave of his time and his formidable intellect for a very gentlemanly duel over the meaning of *Showto Na Slavi*. Professor Ivailo Ditchev was also an excellent sparring partner both in Sofia and in Istanbul at the Association for Cultural Studies Crossroads Conference in 2006.

No scholarship in any language previously existed on *Showto Na Slavi*. Original primary research, including focus group interviews with Bulgarian audience members, were accomplished in educational settings (at a high school, technical college, and university). Thanks to MediaLinks for sharing their research on *Slavi*'s audience with us. We were also able to interview one of the creators of *Showto Na Slavi*, Lyuben Dilov Jr., as well as most of the scriptwriters. Our research group, known by us as "Team Slavi," originally consisted of myself, Dr. Iskra Velinova, Daniela Koleva, Anelia Dimitrova, Neli Gogovska, and Yuliyana Gencheva. The Bulgarian members of the team had already viewed many dozens of episodes before the date in 2003 that we sat in the studio audience to watch it being filmed. In my living room in Grand Forks, North Dakota, we watched many of the 2003 shows together (along with some English subtitled episodes generously supplied to us by BTV), with some members of the Bulgarian research team informally and cheerfully translating them for my edification. Much sharing of ideas and merriment ensued.

The Fulbright Award also provided a perch in Europe for easier travel to Belgium for some final research into *Jan Publiek*. Iskra Velinova also traveled to the United States on a Fulbright and was able to make it to Grand Forks, where she had the best meal west of the Mississippi at Sanders Restaurant, resurrected downtown after the 1997 flood.

An earlier European perch was had courtesy of the American College of Thessaloniki (ACT), which hosted me for a semester in Greece in the spring of 2001. Many thanks to Eva Kanellis for arranging this. Dr. Anna Challenger, then the extraordinary chair for ACT's English department, was a most benevolent boss. Marianthi Makri-Psilipakou, a professor of sociolinguistics at Aristotle University, has also been an important sounding board through these years. During my first stay in Thessaloniki, my colleague Dr. David Marshall was visiting Veliko Turnovo on his third Fulbright. His invitation and my proximity to Bulgaria resulted in my first trip to that country and my introduction to *Showto Na Slavi*. His mentoring of four Bulgarian graduate students resulted in their admission to UND's English department, and the opportunity for me to write them into a grant for work on *Showto Na Slavi*.

Another lucky coincidence brought Magda Michielsens and Sonja Spee to the Feminisms and Rhetorics Conference in Minneapolis in October of 1999, where I was chairing their panel and presenting a paper on the *Oprah Winfrey Show*. We made a vow to meet at the University of Antwerp, should I ever make it to Europe.

At the Women's Studies Center in Antwerp, now defunct but then headed by Professor Michielsens, her graduate students Sonja Spee and Nico Carpentier had already done fieldwork at VRT on *Jan Publiek*, interviewing the production team and receiving access to VRT's detailed records on each of the panelists. Dr. Carpentier has since published a dissertation in Flemish and two articles in English on his *Jan Publiek* research; he also generously made his knowledge available to me through informal interviews. Dr. Spee's dissertation and published articles on *Jan Publiek* were also in Flemish or Dutch (she is herself Dutch). Spee and I also coauthored a short piece in English for the *European Journal of Women Studies* that bears some similarity to the chapter in this book. It, of course, drew from Spee's fieldwork. Spee and I, together with some other members of the Women's Studies Center, watched the first season's episodes, as our friend Andreas translated our chosen excerpts into English. (Excerpts from the "Migrant Riots" episode were later translated by Dr. Birger Van Wesenbeeck, who came to notice by way of my colleague, Dr. Crystal Alberts.) It is a shame to have lost the Women's Studies Center at the University of Antwerp; much good research and practical activism originated there.

Most of our knowledge of *Oprah* behind the scenes comes from previous research by Jane Shattuc, Laura Grindstaff, Nancy Koehn and Erica Helms, and others. So high is the demand that tickets to the show's taping are difficult to get, to say nothing of contact with the star or staff. We did finally manage the latter and were promised some fact-checking on the *Oprah* chapter, which never materialized. Research assistant Kacie Jossart and I watched many 2006 episodes independently and together, both of us having something more than a studious interest in the program. We coauthored an essay on *Oprah*, part of which I revised for the chapter in this book. Our work was accomplished at the University of North Dakota (and with the help of the Center for Instructional and Learning Technologies), as well as via Internet connection, when I was in Sofia, Bulgaria. Thanks also to the English departments at Louisiana State University and the University of Tennessee for inviting me to speak and permitting me some perspectives on *Oprah* from the southern United States.

The Linguistics Circle of Manitoba and North Dakota provided a knowledgeable audience for an early draft of the Bulgarian study, as did the Fifth and Sixth Fulbright Conferences in Bulgaria. Sofia University Professor Georgi Dimitrov proved a valuable friend and colleague there.

The English Department at UND has always been supportive of this scholarship. Attendees at the departmental faculty lecture series have posed penetrating questions about work on all three talk shows. Many students over the years have likewise offered helpful observations.

Professor Velinova and I are both deeply indebted to Maria Spirova for her negotiations with the Bulphoto Agency, which provided us with still photographs of *Showto na Slavi*.

Thanks to Walter for his perspective on the Flemish language.

I thank my family of origin and D. J. Cooper for insights into working-class culture.

Thanks to Dimitri, Pam, and Efi for some fine times in (for me) a foreign country, thereby rendering it less foreign.

Thanks to my fellow Fulbrighters in Bulgaria for their friendship, with a special nod to Roger Craik, Linda Rashidi, and Sunnia Ko.

I thank my partner Nancy Hennen Longie for her understanding as this long process has come to a close. Her daughters Olivia and Whitney and our dogs Bill and Lucky have not only provided companionship but a grasp on reality that long projects can erode.

Thanks to my niece Rachel for advising me to stop emailing her and finish writing the book!

Without the generosity of all of the institutions and individuals named above, and more that remain unnamed, this book would not have been possible.

~

CHAPTER ONE

Introduction

An important fact of the world we live in today is that many persons . . . live in . . . the multiple worlds that are constituted by the historically situated imaginations of persons and groups spread around the globe. (Appadurai 33)

Cultural productions derive their meaning from the judgments of pleasure and value that audiences make of them. To refuse to make such judgments is to remove oneself from the domain of culture and to place oneself in the domain of science. (Shumway 105)

When Simon Frith (2000) poses the question, "What is good television?" it turns out he means: how is good television "recognized in production practice"? There is no doubt something to be said for sociological mapping of tastes and judgement, but in much of this sort of work, we find that "professional ideologies" are asked to account for such judgements so that sociocultural-educational background does the work of explanation. This renders important issues of authenticity, innovation, creativity and integrity effectively inert because it sees their provenance as merely a matter of birth, education and (mechanistically determined) ideology. Like characters in a Greek tragedy, television's creative personnel are seen as living out predetermined "taste scripts." Where is human agency here? (Jacobs 432)

Now rhetoric returns also as *actio*, as a mode of delivering words, or managing and acting. It is a *performance*, an action that has a not insignificant degree of well worked out artistry. It is the re-emergence of sounds, and not only of sight, that in fact had accompanied the strong development of rhetoric throughout antiquity. This return is also an attempt on the part of our civilization to . . . recover the sensory dimension, the libidi-nal erotic pleasure of the word—its "presence," to borrow a term from a scholar close to McLuhan: Walter Ong. (Barilli 125)

The Global Village Revisited offers something new on the scene of cultural studies and talk show scholarship, both already well developed. This book argues that "good television"—sometimes referred to pejoratively in televi-sion scholarship—might sometimes actually be good, both in the aesthetic and moral sense. Specifically, the argument is that, under certain conditions, highly popular television talk shows can contribute to democratic discourse and do so artfully. This book offers a humanistic methodology, a new rhetoric especially developed for the television talk show, one that combines classi-cal and modern notions of rhetoric with a popular poetics. The interpretive result of this new rhetorical analysis is the identification of what we call a po-litical aesthetic. The book compares the political aesthetic of three different shows from three different countries in the belief that the political aesthetic grows out of specific cultural and historical contexts.

Most talk show scholarship has been social scientific in methodology. Textual analyses of the shows have often dug into the transcripts for their "content," or discursive themes. Recently, talk show scholarship has been influenced by cultural studies. Within that domain, the political has often been narrowed to a focus on production or ideology, the artistry of texts hav-ing been deliberately excluded. Whether grim or celebratory, art and popular culture scholarship within cultural studies tends to be instrumental (Sterne), important primarily for its usefulness to a revolutionary politics. Andrew Tolson's collection *Television Talk Shows: Discourse, Performance, Spectacle* occasionally gestures toward the kind of method needed for a political aes-thetics of television talk shows. Louann Haarman, for instance, performs a discourse analysis of several talk shows that ends with an acknowledgment of television talk's "similarities with forms of TV drama"; such shows "bear the closest resemblance to popular fiction" (63). However, much television scholarship—which overlaps with cultural and popular culture studies—of-ten frames the viewing experience in terms of entertainment, sometimes seen as a degraded experience.

If the thesis regarding "good" television seems overly optimistic, we hope that the book will not be classed among those that breathlessly admire televi-sion and all that is populist. These three "good" shows—one from the United States, one from Belgium, and one from Bulgaria—are also implicated in a range of discourses, many of which we might judge to be far less than salutary. However, to ignore what is good among the bad is, frankly, to engage in a perversity that will never result in a popular political movement. And to presume that television is little more than "the child of an industrial system" (Shattuc 152) is seriously to overstate the very real limitations on agency and creativity that attend such work. Because art and politics are mutually constitutive, cultural critics must develop a means of valuing the kinds of popular art that might conceivably further a democratic politics. The particular type of the television talk show that is treated in this volume—the entertaining yet civic-oriented program—is an excellent place to begin.

That simple description, "entertaining yet civic-oriented," belies the difficulty inherent in the concept. Our three television talk shows attempt in different ways to bring together not just more than one genre (television is famous for its hybridity of genres), but more than one mode of symbolic production, and each of these modes is aimed at a different (although potentially overlapping) audience. Some television talk shows attempt to involve their relatively small, elite audiences in a representation of serious civic matters. Entertainment shows often aim for a larger audience that may even attract members of different social classes. The modes of performance, too, are different. The "talking heads" of many political discussion shows—the phrase itself is indicative of the almost disembodied quality of such programming—may be effectively analyzed in the terms of classical rhetoric, the rhetoric of law (forensic) or politics (deliberative). One might attempt a literary analysis of entertainment shows, since they draw from the many genres of popular art that still today can fit largely into two main categories, that of comedy or drama (often melodrama). Such an analysis would get at the sensuous, affective, and aesthetic experience of popular art. Our study must capture the complex nature of these unusually ambitious television shows.

To get a large audience for talk that is civic-oriented is itself an achievement, and it is what unites the three objects of our study. Otherwise, the shows are refreshingly different. *The Global Village Revisited* compares across subgenres (the afternoon talk show, the evening audience discussion show, and the late-night talk show) and across national boundaries. The assumption underlying the selection of these programs is that each country or region may produce its own type of highly popular, civic-oriented talk show in historical moments that favor such development. Even in an era of extraordinary globalization, the art and politics of the talk show look different from different locales. From the United States comes the long-running afternoon talk show, the *Oprah Winfrey Show*; from Belgium, the prime-time audience discussion show, *Jan Publiek*; and from Bulgaria, the late-night television talk show, *Showto Na Slavi*. The shows represent three very different countries—a capitalist behemoth that may be in decline; a small, and yet still divided, bourgeois welfare state; and an economically struggling postcommunist country. Each show is a product of its own people and its own place in history. We assume that all television programs—indeed, all symbolic productions of whatever sort—are always both political and artful. At the same time, what makes these particular television talk shows unique is their ability to bring together what is often separated: the rhetoric of civic life with the art and entertainment for which the medium of television is generally known.

Talk Shows and Democracy

From a U.S. and Western European perspective, this would seem to be exactly the wrong moment to be uttering "talk shows" and "democracy" in the same breath. The heyday of the issue-oriented talk show is over. *Sally Jesse Raphael, Ricki Lake, Geraldo*—all gone. The inventor of the genre, Phil Donohue, has not been able to make a comeback. *Oprah* (as we shall see) has hybridized the genre yet again, and in the direction of less, not more, studio audience interaction. In the 1980s and 1990s Western Europeans reinvented the issue-oriented talk show to their tastes and cultural backgrounds, but the talk show host Robert Kilroy-Silk has been banished from the BBC airwaves after a seventeen-year stint; the Flemish *Jan Publiek*, treated in this volume, is gone too. In their day, these talk shows also inspired some excellent scholarship on both sides of the Atlantic, most of it centered on the question of whether or how the shows contributed to democratic discourse. But if the time for the issue-oriented television talk show is mainly past, why not just move on to something else?

Originally, the idea was to investigate how ordinary people talk about civic topics on television talk shows. I was more interested in the craft of the talk than were Livingstone and Lunt, Munson, Peck, and Shattuc, but we all—including a number of other talk show scholars, like Andrew Tolson, who said he emphasized "analysis" over [political] "judgment" (24)—were drawn to the concept of the public sphere. We wanted to know how the mass media might be used for democratic ends; for some U.S. scholars, the ends were also feminist (Haag, Masciarotte, Rapping, Shattuc, Squire). Much of this early work was guardedly optimistic about the degree to which ordinary people were getting their say on television. As the television genre itself grew and changed, so did the scholarship. The shows were seen as manipulative of their ordinary guests and of the home audience (Carpentier, Grindstaff, Wood). "Trash" talk shows began to look better than their bourgeois counterparts; they were ironic, they were carnivalistic, and it did not hurt that they were denounced by prigs and bombasts on the right (Gamson; Manga; Shattuc "Shifting Terrain").

Three Shows that Make Political Art

When I traveled to Bulgaria and discovered that the most popular talk show—perhaps the most popular Bulgarian-produced show of any variety—was *Showto Na Slavi*, I began to study it. *Showto Na Slavi* is a different breed altogether, if we follow the already-established framework; it is a "late-night entertainment talk show" marked by its "celebrity chat" (Timberg 7). The creators of the show themselves claimed to be inspired by the U.S. *Tonight Show With Jay Leno*. But tonally, formally, and functionally, the show is quite different. Like its trickster host, Slavi Trifonov, the program is outsized and wild, featuring musical performance, skits, and edgy political satire, all of which regularly reference history, art, and international politics. *Showto Na Slavi* addresses the audience as Bulgarian and citizens of the world. To claim that the show is popular in Bulgaria merely because it has "local content"—an expression from the shortsighted corporate world—would be both an inaccuracy and an understatement, and would also overlook the exceptional artistry of the show, which puts it head and shoulders above most other television fare. Both for its artistic excellence and for its potential contribution to a global public sphere, this is a show that matters.

Jan Publiek (1997–2001)—"John Public"—was a smart audience discussion program, which accomplished and contained its audacious aim of giving voice to ordinary "unknown" Flemings by restraint and careful symmetry. Balance was the keystone of *Jan Publiek's* aesthetics and politics, from the set design to the representative selection of panelists, to the give-and-take of discussion as mediated by the producer-host, the witty, popular, and "well-known" Fleming Jan Van Rompaey. *Jan Publiek* derived from shows like *Het Lagerhuis* ("The Lower House") in the Netherlands and *Kilroy* in Britain (itself influenced by U.S. afternoon issue-oriented talk shows). Yet the program provided to its sizeable audience something uniquely Belgian, uniquely Flemish, in a television schedule that offered much foreign programming. Belgians see themselves as quiet, overlooked, but nevertheless essential, actors on the world stage. Although not prone to protest, Flemings have had to fight for the use of their language in their own country. During the run of *Jan Publiek*, Flemings were front and center stage, speaking in their language (not French) and from their city of Antwerp (not Brussels). The "unknown"

Flemings became "well known"—at least for a season, when a new group was ushered in—and provided some delightfully democratic television fare. The last third of our Flemish case study takes us to more difficult territory, as the show's balance and symmetry were put to the test by the "Migrant Riots" episode.

The *Oprah Winfrey Show* is the grande dame of the U.S. afternoon talk show genre that continues to earn high audience ratings despite the proliferation of programs and channels after the advent of cable and satellite television, and despite its own advanced age. At twenty-two, the show is an exemplar of intelligent adaptation amid the global flows, to which the U.S. "media imperialists" are themselves subject (the show is seen, by the way, in 122 countries, according to oprah.com). The host is herself a fascinating and world-renowned presence who has discovered how to make the traps and trappings of celebrity work to her advantage. Careful attention to the niche (mainly female and middle-class) audience has kept it large and loyal. The new *Oprah* invites the audience into indulgent fantasies, often centering on the world of celebrity, but still maintains its commitment to quotidian melodrama and, more surprisingly, to an invocation of the audience as citizen. It has merely institutionalized this in new ways.

Television talk shows, then, do not cease to be of interest to cultural or television studies. Rather than universalize through our use of generic epithets like "issue-oriented," we might try to see how a show functions within its own cultural and historical milieu. Just because something is not happening in the United States or the Anglophone world (around which most talk show scholarship centers) does not mean it is not happening. Nor has commercial television necessarily become antithetical to usefully political programming—although we do admit that it generally has. The *Oprah Winfrey Show* is more and more clearly politically liberal, and very useful to the call by British leftist Colin Sparks to strengthen the state (93). *Showto Na Slavi*, Bulgarian born and bred, is also sharply political, but so far has not suffered from its owner, Balkan News Corp, a subsidiary of Rupert Murdoch's News Corp. Nor does the "manipulation" of any of these shows' participants, whether ordinary people or celebrities, signify something darkly antidemocratic. No matter what the medium, few will spend their time listening to dull speakers or performers. The left needs to understand the function of art and entertainment as well as the technologies of the electronic media. As well, Anglophone first-worlders need to see how the rest of the world works with these media, as history unfolds in new and unexpected ways. Others' ideas may inspire us.

The Global Village

While highly innovative and "hypermediated" (Bolter and Grusin), television itself may be a poor medium for analysis in general; it tends to disable our senses of history and cultural specificity in favor of an intense yet vague "participation" in "the global village," as Marshall McLuhan taught us more than a generation ago (McLuhan 23 and passim; Marchand 194). His ideas are enjoying something of a comeback (Eco, Paglia, Genosko, Gerrie). McLuhan's theory built on that of Lord and Parry and Erik Havelock, who identified oral cultures as producing different kinds of consciousness in their inhabitants. According to this view, which follows a line of development through Western culture, Attic Greeks experienced the first challenge to consciousness, divided as it was between oral and written "cultures." McLuhan thought that the late twentieth century marked another "crisis," as he put it in *The Gutenbergy Galaxy*, or a transition from print to electronically influenced consciousness—a division between "typographic man" and "graphic man." McLuhan's student, Walter Ong, termed the new consciousness a "secondary orality"—an orality experienced through the electronic media.

For McLuhan, the new consciousness amounted to a "retribalization" of the human community within which "sight and sound and movement are simultaneous and global in extent" (*Gutenberg* 5). It offered "new shapes and structures of human interdependence and of expression" (5). Gutenberg man was linear, inured to compartmentalization, requiring that every last dot get filled in with information. He was perspicuously visual and rational. But now, "[i]t is a matter of 'rite words in rote order,' as Joyce put it. [McLuhan believed that artists were the first to adumbrate transitions to new phases of human history.] [A]ny Western child today grows up in this kind of magical repetitive world as he hears advertisements on radio and TV" (19). "Electronic man" prefers "cool" media, which require him to fill in some of the meaning, to participate. Biographer Philip Marchand glosses McLuhan's "cool" as "enigmatic, playful, absorbing" (277).

Things may not be quite as bad as Lewis Lapham, interpreting McLuhan, suggests ("Like the nomadic hordes wandering across an ancient desert in search of the soul's oasis, graphic man [i.e., the television viewer] embraces the pleasures of barbarism and swears fealty to the sovereignty of the moment" [xxiii]), but there is some truth to what he is saying. We can see it better when Lapham says that McLuhan's theory of the difference between "typographic/print man" and "graphic/electronic man," "accounts . . . for the triumph of Madonna and Rush Limbaugh" (xxii). Similarly, McLuhan biographer Philip Marchand updates a McLuhan aphorism: "'The politician will be only too happy to abdicate in favor of his image, because the image will be so much more powerful than he could ever be.' McLuhan did not quite live to see the Age of Reagan and the full vindication of that statement" (219).

McLuhan's aphorisms sometimes clarified things too much, and his ideas were overapplied, without regard to the nuances and caveats—not to mention the outright contradictions—in his work. In his best-known book, *Understanding Media*, he lauds the CBC broadcast of Glenn Gould's piano recitals: "A cool [i.e., participatory] medium, when really used, demands this involvement in process" (31). I myself enjoy watching the U.S. cable-funded C-SPAN, especially the program "Book TV," which is no more than people talking about their books, often depicted in medium shot by a couple of stationary cameras. Unless one is interested in the ideas being conveyed, the "show" is as dull as dull can be. Television, when used well, is "tactile," in McLuhan's idiom, meaning that it involves all the senses: it is not emotionally distancing, it is not only visual (when cameras move and swoop to create excitement, they are not merely visual), or even only auditory (I do not mind listening to Book TV with my eyes closed), and it does not segment consciousness the way that "book culture" tends to do. McLuhan can explain my perverse "participation" in Book TV:

> To literary people, the practical joke with its total physical involvement is as distasteful as the pun that derails us from the smooth and uniform progress that is typographic order. Indeed, to the literary person who is quite unaware of the intensely abstract nature of the typographic medium, it is the grosser and participant forms of art that seem "hot," and the abstract and intensely literary form that seems "cool." "You may perceive, madam," said Dr. Johnson, with a pugilistic smile, "that I am well-bred to a degree of needless scrupulosity." (32)

That the above commentary has class implications is never mentioned by McLuhan, who despised Marxism, but surely it does, because some of the "pre-Gutenberg man" still lives in rural, working-class, and postcolonial people. Indeed, it lived in McLuhan, who was known for his puns. It lives in all of us who enjoy the bawdy humor and melodrama found in all three of our talk shows. The contradictions within McLuhan's ideas may well spring from the division of his own allegiances. He took two degrees from Cambridge, as a highly successful "typographic man" might well do, but he was drawn to early (pre- and Renaissance) literature as well as to the works of William Blake, James Joyce, and Ezra Pound: in other words, literature that still seems strange to many.

I will return later to McLuhan's mention of "forms of art," for one line of argument in this book is that ordinary plebeian television can be artistic.

Here, we will want to note that the recent tradition of talk show scholarship has often rested upon exactly the notion of "participation" that seems antithetical to a "cool" medium—that is, Habermas's highly rational—and idealistic—notion of discussion in the public sphere. Ideas have perhaps never been shorn of performance, but certainly, in the age of television, if our "village" is a global one, it will offer a participatory experience, and one rather different from that of public sphere theory. The kind of emendation of Habermas's bourgeois public sphere to something more "inclusive" is also inadequate from the point of view of creative expression. To say that democratic discourse should be "inclusive" or "nondominating" (Young) is in one sense self-evident, but from another perspective such requirements seem to invite a paltriness we would not like. M. M. Bakhtin's notion of carnival would seem to be out of place there, since carnival laughter is "ambivalent: it is gay, triumphant, and at the same time it is mocking, deriding. It asserts and denies; it buries and revives" (12). Some of this rough-and-tumble world makes its way into our talk shows.

Arjun Appadurai corrects McLuhan's metaphoric use of "village": "We are now aware that with media, each time we are tempted to speak of the global village, we must be reminded that media create communities with 'no sense of place'" (29). This is important, for to be involved emotionally or "tactilely" (in McLuhan's coinage) is not the same as actually experiencing the world that is represented on television. As well, since McLuhan's time, television programming is answerable more and more to worldwide media moguls; they are the ones who—from a very distant perch—are representing that world. Although local programming continues and in some places still achieves some prominence (Wang and Servaes), funding for local media production, including European public television—sometimes the only "local" outlet—is diminishing (Chalaby). And although it may seem that the United States is exempted from this situation, since the great majority of its programming originates in the United States and is in English, still, most programming is created in just a few media capitals (Curtin, Chalaby). When regions are represented—as was rural Arkansas recently in Paris Hilton's *The Simple Life* (see Dixon and Koleva)—they are represented by outsiders. This points to more than just neglect of the local; it means that most programming offering "the world" to us is merely touristic. There is some good news in that the multinational corporations that own most of television have at least (and at last) learned to "localize," usually by planting local bases in individual countries or regions that share a language, but feeding plenty of dubbed or subtitled nonlocal (often U.S.-produced) programming to their viewers (Chalaby, Sinclair, Straubhaar). This does, of course, vary by region.

The U.S. media do not enjoy hegemony in Asia nor in South America—in fact, Mexican media export to U.S. Hispanics (Straubhaar and Duarte; Lee). Our television talk shows make their origins known. The experience of watching our one program in worldwide syndication, the *Oprah Winfrey Show*, appears to be utterly different from outside the United States (Wilson) and, in my experience, the viewing experience varies by region of the United States as well.

The time is nigh for the development of a global public sphere (Sparks), however imperfect. It would be adapted to a new media environment, but to move in that direction we would need much more knowledge of one another than mainstream television currently offers. Especially when I think of *Slavi*, I am also moved to wonder whether Appardurai's "diasporic public spheres" might be apt, since in the case of Bulgaria and its emigrants, "both viewers and images are in simultaneous circulation" (4). Taken altogether as examples of very popular programs, *Slavi*, *Jan Publiek*, and *Oprah* can show us how to address large audiences successfully. This is even more crucial now, since it is harder than ever to draw such audiences. Even within our own countries, the advent of niche programming has meant that we are less likely than in the days of early television to watch the same television programs as others outside of our group, whether defined by class, age, sex, ethnicity, and other identifying characteristics (Straubhaar).

Until recently, scholars seem to have been likewise afflicted. The preface to a 1996 collection on regional television flows points out that both American and European television scholarship is self-absorbed and insular (Sinclair et al. v). Three editors and nine authors cover six regions that touch upon every earthly continent. *The Global Village Revisited* will delve more deeply but across a more limited geographic range, one that shares, to some extent, a cultural heritage, the Americas having once been "Old" Europe's "New World." Even so, the differences among these countries are substantial. The study deliberately foregrounds two small countries. One of them, Belgium, is sandwiched between the two superpowers France and Germany and is subdivided into three linguistic and relatively autonomous political regions. One of those regions, the newly prosperous Flanders, shares its language, more or less, with The Netherlands, comparatively larger and more powerful. The other small country featured in *The Global Village Revisited* is Bulgaria. From the Middle Ages onward, Bulgaria has often been the pawn of Western and near-Eastern powers, and today ranks among the poorer countries of the new European Union. Our inclusion of the U.S. example allows us not only to see what the lowly talk show—lowly on the scale of cultural capital (Mittell 108–20)—is capable of offering within the most favorable of conditions for production and distribution, but also to see what the United States does not seem capable of offering. In terms of popular art and democratic rhetoric, smaller may sometimes be better. Even to be wealthy may not always be the advantage we often believe it to be.

(Re)Building the Nation

Whatever future internationalism may have, it is still the case that nationalism is the means through which the international is both materially and imaginatively taken up by people the world over. As Homi Bhabha put it, almost twenty years ago now,

> Nations, like narratives, lose their origins in the myths of time and only fully realize their horizons in the mind's eye. . . . This is not to deny the attempt by nationalist discourses persistently to produce the idea of the nation as a continuous narrative of national progress, the narcissism of self-generation, the primeval present of the *Volk*. Nor have such political ideas been definitively superseded by those new realities of internationalism, multi-nationalism, or even "late capitalism," once we acknowledge that the rhetoric of these global terms is most often underwritten in that grim prose of power that each nation can wield within its own sphere of influence. ("Introduction" 1)

Each of our television shows is involved in kindling and shaping the nationalist imagination of their respective countries or regions. Although each goes about this project in its own way, faithful to the specific historical conditions of its time and place of origin, they all share the discourse of nationalism to which Bhabha refers. Sometimes the discourse does indeed seem "grim," as Bhabha says; sometimes not.

Ernest Gellner argues that "nationalism is, essentially, the general imposition of a high culture on society, where previously low cultures had taken up the lives of the majority, and in some cases of the totality, of the population" (57). This high culture appeared in late eighteenth-century Western Europe as a result of industrialization, which required a rationalized systematization of both the economy and the state, as well as mobilization of the work force. The resultant emphasis on unity and efficiency and uprooting of the populace forged a new political unit that was based on ethnic sameness and/in an invented nationalism. This nationalism rose out of one or more of the original cultures of the geographical area, but was virtually unrecognizable in its new form, therefore the inventedness of nationalism. It relies on state education—and, we would add, the media (see Dhoest, "Reconstructing" 6)—for its continual renewal. Its (relatively) new loyalties are not deep rooted in some ancient past, but rather are a modern historical necessity.

Benedict Anderson argues that it remains to explain how and why people are so attached to their national identity. First, one needs to understand that nations are "imagined communities" (6). These are imagined communities because the members are joined by their imaginations, rather than through face-to-face encounters, but nonetheless are communities because there is in fact "a deep horizontal comradeship" (7). The binding power of the nation was necessary to replace the previous social and spiritual glue of "the *religious community* and the *dynastic realm*" (12): "What I am proposing is that nationalism has to be understood by aligning it, not with self-consciously held political ideologies, but with the large cultural systems that preceded it, out of which—as well as against which—it came into being" (12). Before nationalism,

> [h]uman loyalties were necessarily hierarchical and centripetal because the ruler, like the sacred script, was a node of access to being and inherent in it. Third was a conception of temporality in which cosmology and history were indistinguishable, the origins of the world and of men essentially identical. Combined, these ideas rooted human lives firmly in the very nature of things, giving certain meaning to the everyday fatalities of existence (above all death, loss, and servitude) and offering, in various ways, redemption from them. (36)

In our analyses of television talk shows, the clearest example of nationalism-as-depth can be found on *Showto Na Slavi*, which closes every episode with the same ritual gestures.

Rehearsing the development of nationalism is helpful because our three countries are so different in their ascriptions of nationalism. Anderson casts the United States as one of the leaders in developing the contemporary political form of nationalism, but Western Europe was soon to follow, and to engage in building nations that were culturally different from the United States. Gellner's notion of the ethnically distinct composition of nation—even if it is "the new, educationally-transmitted ethnicity" (86)—suits Western Europe well. Anderson accounts for the U.S. version of nationalism better. Certainly the Euro-Americans strove to dominate and even eliminate some non-European groups; however, the size of the African American (originally slave) population and the many immigrant groups, including Hispanic Americans in the Southwest and Asian Americans along the West Coast, was simply too massive, widespread, and culturally diverse ultimately to control. The mythology of the "melting pot" was created to describe a process of national acculturation:

> At the beginning of this century, as steamers poured into American ports, their steerages filled with European immigrants, a Jew from England named Israel Zangwill penned a play whose story line has long been forgotten, but whose central theme has not. His production was entitled "The Melting Pot" and its message still holds a tremendous power on the national imagination—the promise that all immigrants can be transformed into Americans, a new alloy forged in a crucible of democracy, freedom and civic responsibility. (Booth A1)

Different groups of immigrants and ethnicities responded differently to the melting pot myth—that is, to acclimation to the dominant culture (Ogbu)—and the myth was assuredly employed by the dominant groups as a means of absorbing difference. Nonetheless, the myth points to a characteristic of U.S. nationalism that differentiates it from the Western European variety: however many spaces might be found for people of color (myths of the melting pot or multiculturalism, as well as actual, and sometimes ghastly, places: Indian reservations, sharecropping huts, big-city tenements, internment camps), spaces must be made. The struggles between dominant and marginal groups were apparent from the outset of nationhood, as Indian peoples and African slaves were differentially written into the Constitution; later, Indian wars, the Civil War, and the Mexican-American War were fought to wrest territory from those who would not "melt" away. Colonialism was not practiced so much on foreign lands as at the center of one large continent ("from sea to shining sea"). Large though it was, the United States was never large enough, or—considering the size of European nation-states—small enough, to pretend to utter sameness.

Behind the coercive myth of the melting pot lay horrific violence but also at certain historical moments and to varying degrees, an acknowledgment that difference went into the makeup of "American" identity, and continues to do so. The first person of color was elected to the presidency in 2008, an event that many believe would be unlikely in a Western European nation (see National Public Radio, "Obama Election"). On the other hand, that event might seem like a miracle, following hard on the heels of the disastrous aftermath to Hurricanes Rita and Katrina, in which hundreds, mostly African Americans, directly lost their lives (Brinkley 621). It is this episode of American life that prompted the usually centrist *Oprah Winfrey Show* to take a stand for liberalism—that is, the position that government has a constructive and substantial role to play in the lives of its citizens.

There is one more point to make with regard to U.S. nationalism. Although the identification with other Americans is not necessarily based on ethnicity, its nationalism is nevertheless a strongly binding agent. It has engendered the belief in "American exceptionalism."

> The pre-historicist idea of the United States as a special case "outside" the normal patterns and laws of history runs deep in American experience. Its origins, Dorothy Ross shows, lay in the merger of the republican and millennial traditions that formed an ideology of exceptionalism prominent in American historical writing. In this liberal world view, the United States avoided the class conflicts, revolutionary upheaval and authoritarian governments of "Europe" and presented to the world an example of liberty for others to emulate. (Tyrrell 1031)

It is perhaps this belief in American exceptionalism that makes it possible for the United States to behave so truculently around the world, while maintaining an innocent, even virtuous, self-image.

Although Bhabha borrows from Frantz Fanon, unlike Fanon, Bhabha is not interested in the building of a nation after colonialism, or after other forms of subjugation. Bhabha's project is a deconstructive one that reads the contradictions of nationalism against itself, particularly its always partially failed attempts to inscribe a unified culture, ethnicity, and rooted past. Alexander Dhoest takes up a similar project in his work on Flemish period drama, the "predominant domestic fiction genre on Flemish television" from the early 1960s through the late 1980s ("Quality" 305). He points out, for example, "the broadcasters' middle-class version of the Flemish past" ("Quality" 320). This particular mediated image of the Fleming is also made to be ethnically distinctive in period fiction:

> One of the prime national myths concerns the so-called "Battle of the Golden Spurs" on 11 July 1302. Under the influence of novelist Henri Conscience, author of The Lion of Flanders (De Leeuw van Vlaanderen, 1838), this battle is seen as an early example of "Flemish" resistance against "the French." However, the current region of Flanders wasn't a political entity at the time and both opponents were ethnically mixed. (Droste, 1993: 69; Morelli, 1996: 181) ("Reconstructing" 4)

Ultimately, these narratives of nationalism arrived at a Flemish character that could occupy the central place in a narrative of struggle against dominating others. In the end, "Flanders evolved from being an 'underdog' to being the dominant community in Belgium" ("Reconstructing" 18).

The serials narrate a nostalgic meta-story, situating the roots of the (then) current Flemish emancipation among the brave country people of the past. Their obstinate, rebellious nature, so the story goes, enabled the Flemish to resist foreign domination and to remain faithful to their roots during centuries of occupation, and their industrious nature allowed to overcome [sic] poverty and to make Flanders into a prosperous region. ("Reconstructing" 10)

Nevertheless, the story of Flanders is not exactly the same as other nationalist narratives, since Flanders has not become a nation. Dhoest refers to Flemish "nationalism" as "cultural emancipation" ("Reconstructing" 3). It is this process of emancipation that *Jan Publiek* rather self-consciously subscribed to. Nevertheless, we can also see in several episodes how the notion of the Fleming does not exactly emancipate all Flemings equally. Even more seriously, there is the problem of whether an immigrant can ever become fully Fleming.

There is, in short, plenty of reason to adopt Bhabha's deconstruction of nationalism. Whenever national unity is seemingly achieved, it occurs at the expense of marginalized "others" but also of everyone's potentially complex ethnic (and other) identifications. It creates strife (sometimes barely concealed) within national boundaries and across them. Nonetheless, for all of the theoriticians of nationalism, and indeed for all of the rest of us, nationalism is simply a given. To use M. M. Bahktin's language, it is an already-existing utterance to which our replies must be made. It is the means of recognition of a people throughout the world, even if it does not represent "the zone of occult instability where the people dwell" (Fanon, quoted by Bhabha, 303). Such a representation would in any case be a difficult matter, scarcely approachable in the analysis of a television talk show. However, the realms of carnivalesque comedy (as in *Showto Na Slavi*) and melodrama (especially as seen in some *Oprah Winfrey* episodes) may bring us to some unstable and expressive moments.

Fanon conceives the project of nationalism differently from Bhabha because he is concerned about shaking off the yoke of colonialism.

A national culture is not a folklore, nor an abstract populism that believes it can discover the people's true nature. . . . A national culture is the whole body of efforts made by a people in the sphere of thought to describe, justify, and praise the action through which that people has created itself and keeps itself in existence. A national culture in underdeveloped countries should therefore take its place at the very heart of the struggle for freedom which these countries are carrying on. (Fanon 233)

Showto Na Slavi, we argue, also takes up the sign of nationalism intentionally, and as a strategy of survival. Bulgarian nationalism has been accomplished only fitfully, most dramatically just before World War I, but more recently during Communism, a period of rapid modernization. At that time, Bulgarian culture became a matter of official concern and deliberate shaping. The performance of elaborate nineteenth-century folk dances, replete with costumes and music, are still a part of what Gellner would call the high culture of Bulgaria, and what government and educational groups offer to tourists and foreign visitors as "Bulgarian culture." It is partly in reply to this rather insular high culture that *Showto Na Slavi* addresses its own version of "Bulgarian," a creation that we imagine to have some similarity to Fanon's "national culture."

Cultural Studies and "Good" Television

We do not think that power is always and only a question of might or money. Skill, wit, and talent remain meaningful qualities, especially but not only in the talk show hosts themselves. What we see when we place our three shows side by side is the variety of good television that has been available in the form of the talk show. Each of the three case study chapters will place the professional biographies of Jan Van Rompaey, Slavi Trifonov, and Oprah Winfrey within the contexts of their eponymous shows and of the cultures and historical moments that they represent. Each of these three hosts has been central to the creation of the talk shows we will analyze; each has an artistic and a political agenda that can be understood as broadly democratic. The creators of these television talk shows all have intended to persuade their audiences to become better citizens, the hosts themselves providing leadership down this path. All three shows have at times even provided fora for ordinary citizens to voice their opinions.

However, the shows have been popular not because they were morally good but because they provided "good" television. Not a few talk show scholars have been tripped up by this last imperative. To some it has seemed that the two definitions of "good" cannot coexist. "The media" was said to "manipulate" its studio audience in ways that might be seen as exploitive at worst, at best distorting of the speaker's intent (Carpentier, Grindstaff). It is true that television is a more heavily layered medium than, say, that of Cicero's "on location" speeches before the Roman Senate. No knowledgeable person, however, can argue that Cicero himself was less manipulating of his audience than talk show producers have been of their "ordinary" guests— and, in a mediated fashion, of their home audiences. Public speaking is a performance; amateurs enter—whether as speaker or as audience—at their own risk. This suggests the need for an educated electorate. *The Global Village Revisited* is but one of many studies that might make a modest contribution to what is now known as "media literacy"—certainly a paradoxical formulation under McLuhan's sign! Viewers of the numerous reality television shows today are often very canny about how the shows are put together, to the point where teenagers with a camcorder or even a cell phone can create their own shows. But if we'd like to move in the direction of literacy, especially critical literacy, something more is needed. "Typographic" and "graphic" "man" are perhaps equally, albeit differently, ignorant. This study admires our chosen television talk shows because they attempt to bring the two poles together.

As we have said, much recent television research has been influenced by cultural studies, an approach that conducts social critique as a means to political justice. But recently a cohort has been building within cultural studies and related areas that wants to enlarge its purview to include art and aesthetics, as Michael Berube's collection titled *The Aesthetics of Cultural Studies* suggests. That collection mainly points the way to future studies, of which, we hope, this book is one. Borrowing from work in cultural and feminist studies, Janet Wolff has also recently argued for the possibility of a progressive aesthetic that could guide art historians and curators in their selection processes. In producing her prolegomena, she brings together politics, ethics, and art—all discourses centering on value. By contrast, Christine Geraghty pioneers work in popular aesthetics by offering a close—and, we think, convincing—reading of the British evening melodrama *East Enders* as a program exhibiting the kind of aesthetic qualities often associated with literature or film. Avi Santo shows how culture, aesthetics, and politics come together in a series of aboriginal television documentaries. Henry Jenkins's most recent book, *Convergence Culture*, argues for the democratic potential of popular art and electronic media that "converge" (i.e., are used in tandem). Although not always rigorous as scholarship, Alan McKee's enthusiastic collection *Beautiful Things in Popular Culture* also makes a contribution to the study of cultural studies and aesthetics.

These beginnings in a new direction nothwithstanding, what cultural studies has been best at, regarding aesthetics, is a critique. Pierre Bourdieu's *Distinction* has been influential in delineating the hierarchy of taste. Jason Mittell's evaluation of television is probably normative. For the most part, we agree with his estimation.

Unlike literature or film, television rarely has pretensions toward high aesthetic value, making it problematic to consider television using the same aesthetic tools designed for high literature or visual arts, because this simply dooms television to evaluative failure and misrepresents the way the majority of television viewers and producers engage with the medium. Similarly, television resists clear authorial definition, with an episodic style of programming and production practices that are even more collaborative than for film, problematizing the authorship models that are evoked in film and literary genre studies. (xiii)

Of course, a lot of programming on subscription channels like HBO and public television resists the above description; as well, films are frequently played on television. My claim, though, is that, like rhetoric, television talk shows can be in dialogue with poetics, drawing from the trove of art and sometimes contributing to it. Furthermore, even though popular aesthetics may differ in some ways from those on high, we should not assume that the overlap may not at times be significant. Authorship on *Slavi*, *Oprah*, and *Jan Publiek* is often in the hands of writers trained in literary or film study, as well as in journalism and television. Authorship also centers on the hosts and their creative vision. Neither Oprah nor Slavi is an auteur exactly, but they are certainly much more than a brand, which would be the corporate expression for their uniqueness. Too often, cultural studies actually follows the corporate lead or repeats the snobbishness of cultural elites.

Theorist David Novitz makes this point too (737), and claims that almost all the distinctions customarily made between "high" and popular art fall away. One that does remain is this: popular art is rarely the expression of a lone genius, but emanates from, and speaks to, "communally instilled values, interests, and beliefs" (742). In this view, art from oral cultures, including the "pre-Gutenberg" European cultures, is all "popular." Adorno and Horkheimer sever past from present popular art with the claim that the current variety no longer bubbles up from the ground of culture but is manufactured from above by capitalists and their ciphers and imposed upon the people, who are known indistinguishably by late capitalism as "the masses." Horkheimer and Adorno evince an appreciation for folk culture, but their desire for rationality and individuality make them better attuned to elite culture; in contemporary art, for Adorno, this was the avant garde. In any event, history for Marx is progressive, or what McLuhan would call "linear." McLuhan's own view of history appears to be circular; the electronic age has begun the process of "retribalizing" us. The artist of McLuhan's televisual medium must draw from communal values even as those values, the medium—and the world itself—change rapidly. Cultural studies scholars have the task of considering all of this within the purview of politics, or social justice, and of doing so more slowly, consciously, and analytically than producers of popular art are likely to do, working at their necessarily hectic pace.

The Art of Rhetoric on the Television Talk Show

The concept of rhetoric comes to us from ancient Greece and Rome, where the term referred to both the actual specific performances themselves as well as a theory or method for studying them. Aristotle called rhetoric "the available means of persuasion" and "the counterpart to poetics." Rhetoricians of both ancient Greece and Rome engaged often in political persuasion, as democratic debate—if not egalitarian democracy—flourished there. Aristotle's formulation reminds us of how closely rhetoric and poetics originally were conceived to be. Rhetoric was an art—that is, a *techne*, or a craft—for producing the speeches for political deliberation, arguments in court, and celebratory events. It was also one of the mainstays of the education of youth, who memorized basic means of reasoning (including the commonplaces), methods of organization (arrangement), and the choices available for style. The latter were impressively elaborated and catalogued by the Romans, especially by the pedagogue Quintilian; these included the figures and tropes that poststructuralist theorists have recently employed for other purposes. Successful speeches were memorized and imitated, but so too was literature, for one of the highest aims of rhetoric was eloquence. Rhetoric, then, could be both craft and art, judged for its effectiveness and for its beauty. It was also judged for its ethical quality. Ethos in classical rhetoric referred to the rhetorician's character—probably the one achieved by reputation but especially the one implied by the performance of the speech itself. Cicero, whose own character was questioned from the times of the late Republic (when he lived) to the present (see Parenti for a Marxist appraisal), nevertheless held high standards for the rhetorician, who, he argued, should be a good man (*On Oratory*). Finally, rhetoric rests on the notion that the address of an audience, specified to a particular time and place, is always centrally important.

Renato Barilli's extension of classical rhetoric to the age of television makes a helpful bridge.

> Now rhetoric returns also as *actio*, as a mode of delivering words, or managing and acting. It is a *performance*, an action that has a not insignificant degree of well worked out artistry. It is the re-emergence of sounds, and not only of sight, that in fact had accompanied the strong development of rhetoric throughout antiquity. This return is also an attempt on the part of our civilization to . . . recover

the sensory dimension, the libidinal erotic pleasure of the word—its "presence," to borrow a term from a scholar close to McLuhan: Walter Ong. (125)

Barilli's words remind us that our talk shows might offer an advance beyond the dull "talking heads" programs by offering—at least at times—this sense of presence. Barilli does not say it, but of the three genres of classical rhetoric—deliberative (legislative rhetoric), forensic (legal rhetoric), and epideictic (ceremonial, or the rhetoric of display)—the latter is perhaps the furthest from logos but the closest to the kind of magic that art can offer. Additionally, its audience was the general population, not just senators or juries. This "praise and blame" genre, spoken at funerals or victory processions, displayed the qualities of the person on whom the speech focused but was itself a display of showy language. Often denigrated as manipulatory or sophistic, epideictic rhetoric has recently been said to provide something essential to the more logos-oriented rhetoric: "'The epideictic auditor is not asked for a judgment . . . but to be a theoros ('witness') to the radiance emanating from the event itself,'" a radiance akin to "the pre-Socratic notion of luminosity, which the Greeks considered 'the stimulus for mental activity'" (Rosenfield, quoted in Rollins, 4). Brooke Rollins ultimately concludes that "the character of presence in epideictic oratory is an action or operation required for all perception"; it is "the condition of possibility of both the forensic and the deliberative genres" (4).

Whether this "presence" is the same quality that McLuhan calls "participation" and that Bakhtin's carnival calls forth in people is debatable. It certainly is the case that Bakhtin cites epideictic rhetoric as a precursor to the medieval carnival that interests him so much: "[I]n the early period of the Roman state the ceremonial of the triumphal procession included on almost equal terms the glorifying and the deriding of the victor" (*Rabelais* 6). Some of what Bakhtin admires about carnival is relevant to what we find in our television talk shows: "their obvious sensuous character and their strong element of play;" that they "closely resemble certain artistic forms, namely the spectacle" and belong "to the borderline between art and life" (*Rabelais* 7). Both *Jan Publiek* and *Oprah* basically operate on bourgeois tastes, and so they incorporate carnival less frequently and in a more muted fashion than does *Slavi*. But the spark is there.

To study the political aesthetic of our three talk shows we must bring together political talk and popular art—and with classical rhetoric. These shows take the overlap among the three even further. All three shows take part in the two large genres of poetics, as set forth by Aristotle—comedy and tragedy (although tragedy becomes melodrama for us moderns). Comedy can take many forms and can appeal to a variety of tastes (Neale and Krutnik). The comic view of life is one that tends to poke fun at people for their foibles and vanities; it may transpire across a narrative with a plot that ends happily. Skits, sketches, gags, and jokes are what Neale and Krutnik refer to as "nonnarrative" comedy. They are generally short-lived and self-contained rather than episodic. Some comedy is mannerly and bourgeois, some carnivalesque.

The comic performances on *Slavi* seem to us to trace a direct lineage to the carnivalesque. Some of the characters that Slavi Trifonov and his troop portray are similar to the typological characters of Harlequin (as seen in commedia dell'arte, Punch and Judy, and so on), and close to the "clowns and fools" that Bakhtin says "stood on the borderline between art and life" (8). We will argue that the morphing character of "Slavi" can also be understood in a mythic register as a trickster figure (Radin), who, in his serious incarnation (generally in the second half of the show), can rightly preside over certain communal rituals. An unusual quality of comedy on the *Slavi Show* is that it is usually comprised of both shorter forms (sketches, etc.) and an overarching narrative. *Jan Publiek* was comprised of a series of shorter dialogues between host and individual panelist. These sometimes took the form of jokes, often set into motion by the lightly satirical host Jan Van Rompaey. On *Oprah*, the comic may work through an hour-long narrative, sometimes crafted like sitcom or a "dramedy," sometimes comprised of gags and other shorter genres. These latter two shows generally give us comedy to the bourgeois taste, but even they include moments of the carnivalesque.

Bakhtin's vision of the world is a comic one, both in the sense of satirizing human foibles and in producing laughter. But as singer/songwriter Joni Mitchell said, "Laughing and crying, it's the same release." Another embodied form of popular art that we find on television talk shows is melodrama. If the democratic nature of comedy is that it shows us all to be small and ordinary despite our pretensions to be otherwise, melodrama makes the most of our seemingly insignificant sufferings. Often the rulers and the ruling class are mocked by comedy; often the plight of the ruled-over is magnified by melodrama. The exaggerated plots and characters of melodrama are "metaphors for 'life's torments' in our culture," as Ien Ang puts it in *Watching Dallas* (64). Melodrama is a modern genre that developed alongside the industrial revolution and the increasing technologization of Western culture because, like Romanticism, it sought to retrieve the human spirit from a ruthlessly mechanized world. Peter Brooks says melodrama reintroduces the moral and spiritual realm by means of a "moral occult." What is felt under modernity is fear and pain that has no precise cause. Melodrama supplies moral clarity by creating heroes, victims (Linda Williams prefers "victim-heroes"), and villains who are all subject to forces that catapult the victims especially into circumstances of extreme physical and emotional peril. That the resolution (often sentimental or "happy") is generally unequal to the gravity and extremity of the preceding exertions only lends to the perpetuation of the need for the genre. Although *Oprah*, as we have said, engages in comedy, melodrama is its favorite choice for the civic-oriented episodes. Melodrama has a long history on *Oprah* and has evolved into a rhetoric that is also a drama, what we will call melodramatic rhetoric.

Both melodrama and "low" comedy, especially, rely upon spectacle as a means of making visible our difficult situation and of encouraging us to see our plight as something shared. In carnivalesque comedy, we "make a spectacle" of ourselves or others. Neal and Krutnik point out that melodrama and comedy "can come surprisingly close, in its concerns as well as in many of its structural features" and can even be found together in one work (13). This is true in the case of our television talk shows, although generally there is some division between the two, whether by episode (the "Migrant Riot" episode of *Jan Publiek* can be seen as melodramatic, whereas most of the other shows from the first season are lightly comic) or by intrapartition (the episode of *Slavi* that we analyze is comprised of a first half that is satiric sketch comedy and a second half that can be sentimental interview. The *Oprah Winfrey Show* offers its viewers both comedy and melodrama, but keeps the two separate. Whenever it moves into overtly political realms, it does so through means of a highly developed melodramatic rhetoric.

Both comedy and melodrama often focus on the sensuousness or physicality and emotionality of life. If Barilli believes that televised rhetoric returns to us something of the "presence" of ancient rhetoric, art critic W. J. T. Mitchell sees something similar being expressed in today's art and entertainment:

> It may be that we are being forcibly reminded by contemporary media that aesthetics (*pace* Kant) can never insulate itself in the pure, disinterested realm of visual pleasure-at-a-distance, but that we inhabit today a sensory environment of accelerating consumption. Bourdieu's insistence that the Kantian criteria of "good taste" are grounded in bourgeois disgust and horror at "vulgar" pleasures of the senses may have a new role to play in an age when both art and mass culture are exploring these sensations under the name of aesthetics. (W. J. T. Mitchell in Bennett et al., 3)

Although Mitchell maintains the notion of a critique of bourgeois tastes (as befits the cultural studies dictionary to which he is contributing), he reminds us that class relations are continually changing. Our television talk shows take part in such changes through their engagement with both "vulgar" and "tasteful." What is surprising about our three television talk shows, however, is the degree to which they combine palpable presence with the more refined elements of logos and ethos. They remain civic-oriented, attempting to construct civic behavior and identities, attempting to persuade to specific political belief or action. They may ridicule satirically and give rise to mocking laughter; they may take us through the abject fears, thrills, sorrows, and sentimentality of melodrama. But, in the process, they always invoke the audience as citizens of a polis that owes something to them but to which they, in turn, owe a debt. This is a new and important form of rhetoric that is simultaneously a new and important form of popular art, one that is potentially inclusive of most members of society, engaging them in a dynamic way. At our historical juncture, it is an achievement of real worth.

Methodology and Method

In putting together our method, we have consulted the work of language philosopher M. M. Bakhtin and rhetorical theorist Renato Barilli. They are both ebullient democrats; both center their theories on language and performance, and both maintain generous views of human possibility. For both, also, art and politics are naturally cohabitant. In the case of Bakhtin, the whole world of meaning is contained in each utterance, no matter how small or no matter the genre. Each utterance takes the form of a speech genre, and is the result of what he calls centripetal and centrifugal forces. They are poised between restrictiveness and freedom, form and openness. Artists may make a great deal more of the form than most of us do, but what anyone of us does with ordinary language is not wholly different: "Bakhtin defines the difference between art and nonart as one of degree, as relational rather than absolute" (Clark and Holquist 208).

Barilli, too, likes to link the artful with the ordinary, but for him the reigning term is rhetoric. In today's world, he says, "elocution [artful delivery of a speech] finds its way in ordinary language, too. The idea that ordinary language is the degree zero of communication, that it is linear, direct, and devoid of rhetorical figures, is no longer acceptable" (127). The way in which speech is formed on television talk shows will be important to us, and not just because it will lead us to understand its ideological content. Indeed, in practice, form and content are never separated, and any theory of language should apprehend this. To see form only as a means of understanding ideological content is to reduce language to something instrumental. This cannot be the way of humanistic research, which must always see art and politics as there together from the beginning.

For Bakhtin, every utterance is simultaneously a form and a worldview—indeed, the form is expressive of the worldview. It will express the speaker's values and perspective every time, and it will do so as part of a social construct. In fact, the utterance itself *is* that social construct in miniature, since it comes into existence in a world of already preexisting language. Every utterance is social and historical, shaped in response to previous utterances and in anticipation of future replies. For Barilli, the art of rhetoric—now extended from expert orator to the speaker of ordinary language, as we have seen—is fundamentally tied to a democratic ethics and an artistry that relies on the audience's plural judgment rather than that of an authoritative mediator (for example, a scholar). The speaker's ethos, or character, is central to the making of meaning in which both speaker and audience engage. For both Barilli and Bakhtin, democratic discourse is a perpetually creative challenge, and, given these two thinkers' sunny dispositions, it is a joyous struggle. There is a robustness to the rhetoric suggested by Bakhtin and Barilli that often moves against the strictures of what Bakhtin called "official discourse" (and this includes, in our day, the discourse of "political correctness"). Bakhtin identifies two main forces shaping all utterances, the dialogic (or openness to otherness, exemplified by the discourse of the novel) and the monologic (seen in the epic and other "closed" genres). Always, the democratic and the antidemocratic will be in dialogue; always there will be a struggle between the two.

Dialogic Speech Genres

Bakhtin's notion of the speech genre and his use of the utterance and genre in the analysis of the novel stand at the center of our method of textual analysis. *Utterance* and *genre* are formally elastic terms in Bakhtin's usage. An utterance, for example, might be one word—as in the case of an exclamation, "Oh!"—or an entire novel. They are also infinitely expandable in the temporal sense, as each utterance or genre (an utterance being accomplished, of course, through genre) is dialogic: it is a response to all relevant previous utterances or genres and it anticipates future replies. If we think synchronically, we can appreciate Bakhtin's desire to see every utterance as an "ideologeme," which expresses "a particular way of viewing the world" ("Discourse" 333). This holism can be "stratified" in order to identify dialects, regionalisms, professional jargons, and folk languages inflected by age, class, and so on.

The rhetorician's sense of audience can be inferred from these aspects of the text. But we also employ J. L. Austin's speech act theory to help us understand the contract between speaker and audience that is struck with every utterance. For Austin, each utterance is a "performative" that has "illocutionary" and "perlocutionary" force:

> [A] locutionary act . . . is roughly equivalent to uttering a certain sentence with a certain sense and reference, which again is roughly equivalent to 'meaning' in the traditional sense . . . we also perform illocutionary acts such as informing, ordering, warning, undertaking, &c, i.e., utterances which have a certain (conventional) force . . . we may also perform perlocutionary acts: what we bring about or achieve by saying something, such as convincing, persuading, deterring, and even, say, surprising or misleading. (109)

If language is a social act, then any given type of utterance or speech genre (to bring Bakhtin back into the mix) always presupposes in the speaker and hearer a shared knowledge of its usual range of meanings. We may not be able to determine the actual success of the perlocutionary act—was the audience persuaded, after all?—but we can at least identify the way in which the audience was invoked. If a very popular television talk show repeatedly invokes the audience in a manner that annoys them, we may assume that the show will not be popular for long—unless indeed annoyance happens to be at the center of the audience's attraction to the show.

Because of our interest in art, we are concomitantly interested in genre as form. Our television talk shows are comprised of a wide variety of speech genres, some of which are quite small (the joke), and some rather large (the melodramatic narrative). The chapters are arranged from short speech genres—*Jan Publiek* was mainly comprised of brief dyadic genres that loosely addressed the evening's stated topic—to longer ones—*Oprah* can sometimes form around an hour-long (though episodic) melodrama. The artistic requirements of the genre play a part in shaping each of these speech genres as they are uttered or filmed. But these requirements do not ever fully determine the utterance, not even in formulaic manifestation, as Jane Shattuc suggests.

> American television is the child of an industrial system, not art. It emanates out of the crafts tradition where skilled workers or corporate professionals produce works that are based on "a body of rules or techniques" much like their Renaissance counterparts. Commercial TV is in a grand tradition of custom production where items are "individually crafted for the purchaser, made singly to discrete specifications" (Scranton, 1997, p. 10). . . . These works are commodities, which are designed in a highly regulated manner, without any background story, to be seen repeatedly to maximize their lives and profits (residues). Once we jettison the belief in the Romanticized artistry of these

works, we can get down to the business of mapping the constraints and under-standing of the possibilities of innovation under the commercial imperative of television. ("Television Production" 153)

Of course, there is a mixture of types here (should the crafts tradition be overlaid with cookie-cutter industrial production?) and a misunderstanding of the possibilities of art (epic and mythic traditions—not to mention the neoclassical movement of the eighteenth century—depended upon repetition and imitation). At the least, the kind of television Shattuc writes about (her example is the U.S. prime-time drama *Law and Order*) should be seen in dialogue with previous television dramas and with speech genres occurring elsewhere on television and in ordinary parlance. It may not be high art, but it speaks to an audience who enjoys seeing how the same basic formula can be worked out in new ways each week. Most of us (if not Romantic artists) are creatures of habit. *Slavi*, for example, exists in dialogue with U.S. late-night talk shows and variety shows and performances from the kritchma (Bulgarian village tavern)—and many more that we will probably never identify (but someone else in the audience perhaps will). To say that *Showto Na Slavi* was just another *Tonight Show* would be folly in the extreme. During the period of our study, the spring and summer of 2003, the show always ended in its own formulaic fashion, which we call ritual. There are few things more deeply meaningful (and less reminiscent of the production line) than ritual. *Slavi*'s producers, writers, and performers were at that time a highly disciplined troop that had been together for a few years. Like any orator, the creative staff of *Slavi* could only anticipate the audience's response, based on what they knew about ordinary Bulgarians. It was never a sure thing that Bulgarians would respond by tuning their television sets to BTV weeknights at 10:30 p.m., but amazingly, one-third of the entire nation did so in 2003 (MediaLinks).

CHAPTER TWO

~

Jan Publiek of Belgium: Flemish Finale

Disembarking at Brussels International Airport, one comes across some declarative signage: "Belgium, the heart of Europe." This claim has credence as Brussels is the seat of a number of important pan-European institutions: the European Commission, the European Union Parliament, and—with intended reach beyond Europe, but expressive of the European form of civilization—the World Court. Brussels is an old city, but a Belgian one only since 1831 when the country was created out of land inhabited by Catholics (in contradistinction to Protestant Holland) that had changed possession many times. It is the capital of Belgium, one of the smallest but most densely populated countries in Europe. Belgium is placed crucially with relation to European superpowers France, Germany, England, and (more modestly) Holland—again, heartlike. A longtime crossroads of trade and capital, Belgium remains a prosperous example of the European genius, a social welfare state grown up from the tragedies of two world wars, surviving now into the twenty-first century (Arblaster). However, historian Tony Judt makes Belgium's fractious story a cautionary tale for all of Europe (701–13). Both the capital city and the country exist under pressure of a global economy and migration from the south and east that are shaping a new Europe. Both are also under threat of radical change by Belgium's northern region, Flanders, which has come dangerously close to seceding. If Belgium is a heart, is it breaking?

Flanders is now the wealthiest and most populous of the two main regions of Belgium. Sandwiched between the main French-speaking part of Belgium Walloonia to the south and Holland to the north, Flanders had long been viewed as rural, Catholic, and backward. In the nineteenth century, Wal-loonia had been a leader in the European drive to industrialize; it was also the dominant force within Belgium. French was the official language used throughout Belgium, and Flemings were forced to learn it if they wished to advance (for example, lectures at Flemish universities were given in French). By the 1920s, a Flemish independence movement was clearly evident and has continued to grow. At present, Vlaams Belang has between 20 and 30 percent of the vote in Flanders, making it the second largest political party in Belgium. One outcome of the independence movement has been the creation of a federalized Belgian state, with each of its parts almost self-governing (this is especially true with relation to cultural and educational concerns; matters of taxation are still decided in plenary).

Central to their claim is the belief among Flemings that their language is distinctive and not merely a dialect of Dutch. In fact, Flemish is spoken in a number of dialects, more than is the case for Dutch. Although grammati-cally Dutch and Flemish are quite similar, a Flemish speaker who has lived in the Netherlands reports that differences in vocabulary and accent cause the Dutch to sometimes misjudge Flemish speakers as German! The "language question" or alternatively "language war" in Flanders is highly developed, not to say esoteric, as well as poignant. My informant says further:

> In a zone about 20–30 miles across the [Flemish-Netherlands] border . . . they speak a nice kind of old Flemish, so that we do not have to adapt at all in that zone. In fact, in that border line, they speak a cleaner Flemish than the Flemish integrationists would have us ever to speak again. Those border Dutch people (northern Brabanders) have gotten of course a clear Dutch accent and use the stereotyped Dutch vocabulary, but they have an old Flemish grammar that we are forbidden to use in public by our own language purists. Sometimes it feels like coming home for us.

Vlaams Belang is known, especially outside of Flanders, as a "right-wing, anti-immigrant" party that agitates for a separate Flanders. But if it had not been judged racist and deliberately circumscribed by a coalition of all the other Flemish (and Belgian) parties, it might be in the driver's seat in Flan-ders (the opposite could be argued—that prohibitions enhance the desire for Vlaams Belang). The sentiments behind the separatist movement are in any case powerful. Similar to northern and southern Italy, the Flemish and Wal-loonian economies have diverged. Walloonia is postindustrial and depen-dent on aid from the Belgian welfare state. From the Flemish point of view, these are handouts taken directly from the pockets of the Flemish taxpayers, who are comparatively well heeled. However, Flemings are not necessarily the masters of their fate, as most Flemish companies have been subsumed by, or subcontracted to, multinationals. The Belgian welfare state is itself rarely able to intervene effectively in labor disputes. But Flemings have by and large adapted well to the global economy.

Since 1999, the far left has been in ascendancy, recently allying with the "allochthon" population, mainly immigrants living in the larger cities (in Brussels, they comprise the majority). Immigration has largely come from two Muslim countries, Morocco and Turkey, by relatively poor people. Come to Western Europe to earn a better living—and, from the Europeans' perspective, to provide once-needed labor in lower-skilled occupations—they are now often displaced from those jobs, many of which have been outsourced. Second-generation allochthons tend still to remain among their own kind; in Flanders, this means often not learning the Flemish language. Fully 40 percent of the children in the Antwerp public schools cannot speak Flemish. Not just the language but the mores and modes of public interaction are severely tried. The Flemish ethnics embody much that the new immigrants—who may have dual citizenship in Morocco and Belgium, or no Belgian citizenship at all—resent: individualism (there is a new contentiousness concerning the inclusion of women in the public sphere), materialism, and secularity (but a secularity built on a definite Christian past). For over two hundred years, the democratic institutions of Western Europe have thrived on critique and change, but change on this order was never envisioned.

Flemish Television

The history of Flemish television is complex, the French-speaking and Flemish-speaking portions of Belgium having rather different histories, even though all of Belgian television was publicly funded until the late 1980s, when "Belgium became one of the most densely cabled countries in the world" (d'Haenens 150). That did not change the desire for programs in the Flemish language, which had been provided ever since the beginning of Belgian television in the 1950s, but at first under the aegis of the unified Belgian state. By the time that *Jan Publiek* was broadcast in 1997, not only had a separate Flemish public broadcasting charter been issued, the original name of the most prominent public station had been changed from BRT 1 to VRT 1—the name reflecting the change in allegiance from the Belgian state to the Community of Flanders (or Vlaanderen, in Flemish). By then, the Flemish audience that wanted programs in their own language could select from two local public and two local commercial (but heavily government-regulated) channels plus three Dutch public channels. About twenty-five channels became available through cable, mostly public but also commercial television stations from other Western European countries, and some commercial stations from the United States as well (MTV, CNN).

Although it has since rebounded to claim the number one spot, there were real worries in 1997 when *Jan Publiek* was first broadcast as to whether VRT could compete with the new commercial channels, even with its combination of state subsidies and newly gained revenue from advertising. Unlike commercial television, the public variety was tasked with providing reliable news, educational programming, and "healthful entertainment for all sections of the population" (VRT 1997). One of the strategies for competition was to make public television more like commercial television. *Jan Publiek* was created in this vein, borrowing from Jan Van Rompaey's previous talk shows, but also from foreign public and commercial programs.

Jan Publiek and Jan Van Rompaey

Jan Van Rompaey, the host and creator of *Jan Publiek*, is a major Flemish television personality, a features journalist, talk show host, and producer whose career has been long and distinguished. In 1967 he contributed to a television magazine program called *Echo*, one of the first Flemish television shows to feature ordinary people, which it did in a fresh, ironically humorous way. A number of scenes and episodes from *Echo* have become classic television for Flemings. In 1973 Van Rompaey was the host of *Terloops* ("In Passing" or "By the Way"), another light, satirical television magazine, this time starring its host and his (usually brief) interviews or interactions with ordinary Flemings. It was broadcast for eleven years. By this time, television viewers considered Van Rompaey a proven performer, and tended to follow him from show to show. During the 1980s and 1990s he experimented with various talk show formats in which he interviewed both ordinary and eminent Flemings.

As an interviewer, Van Rompaey is highly skilled and improvisational, preferring the light touch but well able to insert himself into cacophony and controversy, if the situation so requires. He comes across as bright, well prepared, witty, and engaged. By the time of his retirement in 2005 at the age of sixty-five, he had won numerous awards, being named Best TV Personality or runner-up by the entertainment magazine *Humo* every year the contest was held. Upon his retirement, VRT 1 ran a retrospective of his career for several consecutive Sundays during prime-time titled *SuperJan*. It was fitting that his work be celebrated in this way, for Van Rompaey was important in the shaping of Flemish consciousness, helping to craft a public language and a form of intelligent entertainment that could more than compete in his countrymen and -women's eyes with the Dutch media that was then dominant in Flanders.

Jan Publiek seems a natural outgrowth of Van Rompaey's talents and preoccupations. Indeed, it marks the high point of his contribution to a new Flemish consciousness, an audience discussion show where the majority of the talk was accomplished by a panel of twenty previously unknown Flemings, carefully chosen to be representative of their fellow citizens, and able to remain together as a group for a sixteen-week season. Other audience discussion shows had been created elsewhere. Perhaps the nearest in concept to *Jan Publiek* was a program from Holland titled *Het Lagerhuis* ("The Lower House") in which ordinary Dutch people debated serious topics as though they were sitting in parliament. In England, former MP Robert Kilroy-Silk had gathered fellow Britons together in a more casual way onstage, moving freely among them to ascertain their opinions on a variety of topical questions. In the United States, afternoon talk shows had evolved a format that put a small group of ordinary people and experts before a studio audience that was itself actively addressed by an often-charismatic host. Even more than in the Western European varieties, the American shows tended to highlight feelings, in keeping with the "feminine" afternoon time slot.

Van Rompaey and his coproducers planned an evening show that would feature Van Rompaey as mediating host before a panel of ordinary Flemings who would be prompted to offer their feelings and opinions on issues of the day. The producers studied foreign shows, including some of the over-the-top Americans ones like *Jerry Springer*—abhorrent to Van Rompaey—and sifted through advice from other television professionals, including one who warned that the heady experience of being on air might tempt the panelists to open rebellion. But Van Rompaey held to his democratic aims, inviting the same set of panelists to an entire season of sixteen episodes, enabling them to form a kind of community together, and allowing the home viewers the chance to cleave to them as characters in a continuing narrative, however lightly limned. During the first season—the one that we analyze—they would speak on topics as diverse as dieting, public nudity, and immigrant riots in Brussels.

In creating *Jan Publiek*, Van Rompaey also consulted a study by the Commission of Affirmative Action of the VRT. In it, the researchers concluded that women were underrepresented in most of the Van Rompaey talk show corpus (Michielsens 1991). He had already hosted two talk shows for VRT, the most recent of which had been titled *Schermen*, or *Screens*, a reference both to television screens and to the screens used in the sport of fencing. An often-made feminist argument is that women, having been relegated to the private sphere for centuries, are generally less well oriented toward "fencing" than are many men. There is a bit of the "high" cultural connotation here as well. Something of the aesthetic of *Schermen* carried over to *Jan Publiek*. One senses in the host a man who is both democratic and aristocratic, a gentleman and a television broadcaster, so to speak. It is possibly for this reason—that Van Rompaey embodied both—that class differences were not overtly considered by the show's producers as they selected panelists. In any case, the title of *Jan Publiek*, or John Public, is hardly gender-neutral, but otherwise the show's producers strove to represent women and men equally on the program. Van Rompaey himself said the following:

> We had argued that we have to have 10 men and 10 women. Everybody agreed that, eh, although of course you could—if you are looking for quality in all possible directions—then you probably have to drop [this criterion], but we did not. We were convinced that 10 men and 10 women were self-evident. (Van Rompaey)

The panel, then, consisted of those ten men and ten women who discussed a wide range of topics during the sixteen episodes of the first season. It was broadcast live once a week during prime-time for a variable length, between an hour or two. Selection for the panel began in June of 1997, when the production team launched a national call (via television, radio, and newspapers) for candidates to participate in a panel of "ordinary people." The candidates had to complete a motivation form and a short curriculum vitae, and they were subjected to a discussion test in front of the production team. The final twenty members for the first season were chosen from a pool of 220 candidates. Beforehand, the research center of the VRT had created an ideal panel profile, based on socio-demographic criteria and communication skills (VRT-studiedienst 1997). They determined that the ideal panel should consist of ten men and ten women, of people from different age groups (three above fifty-five years of age, seven between thirty-five and fifty-four, eight between eighteen and thirty-four, and two between fifteen and seventeen), and of people from diverse occupational and educational background (students, one unemployed person, two housewives, workers, retired persons, self-employed people, employees, a businessman). The ability to speak clearly and to express strong opinions cogently was important as well, as were spontaneity and a telegenic presence.

The ideal profile stipulated that two-thirds of the panel be ordinary people ("with whom the audience at home can identify themselves"). The other one-third should be comprised of striking personalities (e.g., a more philo-sophical character, a liberated woman, a real businessman) with remarkable or even headstrong opinions. Other qualities represented among the panel-ists finally chosen included the following: two were women of an ethnic ori-gin that was not Flemish, three were youngsters (twenty-one and younger), two were older than seventy, two were gay men, and others represented the political spectrum from left to right. In the Flemish press, this panel was re-ferred to as "Little Flanders," alluding to its representational nature.

So, in January of 1997, an audacious experiment in television broadcast-ing began: a live, prime-time Flemish audience discussion show featuring panelists that actually drew a following—the "unknown Flemings" of the introductory episodes became the "known unknown Flemings" by the finale. Van Rompaey had worried that the ordinary Fleming panelists might clam up, unlike the more garrulous Dutch on *Het Lagerhuis*. However, the panel-ists had more to say than time would allow. An academic critic, Nico Car-pentier, wrote that on *Jan Publiek* "opinions stay fragmented and can rarely be articulated." He quoted Livingstone and Lunt: "Without pleading for the Habermasian ideal of a 'rational discussion leading to a critical consensus' (Livingstone and Lunt, 1996: 160) in a talk show, it should be noted that a swift succession of isolated statements hardly resembles any discussion at all" (Carpentier 2001, 223). Carpentier later told me that he wondered whether his criticisms might have put an early end to *Jan Publiek*, a show that was composed so carefully, and with critics in mind even on the drawing table.

But the art that was *Jan Publiek* was something quite specific; Habermas does not immediately come to mind. *Jan Publiek* was genial—comic, in the large sense of that term. The view of the citizen that it inscribed was polite, middle-class, self-controlled, and, while admitting of some variety, nonethe-less fairly homogeneous. The society that was implied thereby was a rela-tively coherent one, one that *could* be comic in its disagreements rather than strife-torn. Jan Publiek might be an individual citizen, but he (and, indubi-tably, she) was willing to balance his views and desires with those of other Jans and Janas, and this he could afford to do in good-humored fashion. In fact, it seems clear that Jan or Jana would not normally expect to stand out in the crowd too far above anyone else. Dialogue and not grandstanding was the order of the day. There were certain bedrock shared values. Obviously, there was a belief in a kind of forward progress that Flanders was seen as part and parcel of. This forward movement was balanced and orderly; decency toward one's fellow citizens mattered. Part of the sense of balance was worked with through ideals of fairness and egalitarianism. Despite the strong emphasis on individual striving, there was a sense of communality, of a people sharing a way of life. *Jan Publiek* was optimistic and lively, gentle and wry. Its aims were modest: to provide a forum for ordinary Flemings that would constitute a light entertainment, and beyond that (perhaps this was unconscious) to solidify a Fleming identity that Jan and Jana could be proud of.

It certainly is the case that the format of *Jan Publiek* did require the "Super-Jan" that was Jan Van Rompaey. He brought his decades of experience, and his loyal audience, with him. As host, he was positioned center stage. He introduced the show and its topic, posed the questions to the panelists, and called on them to speak, teacher-style. As is typical of classroom discourse, transitions in turn taking were handled by him (Cazden)—with the exception of portions of the immigrant riots episode, which we will examine later. The result was a clean and crisp show featuring ordinary people who were not trained television professionals. The ordinary Fleming counterparts at home liked it. Audience share for the period that we will treat in this chapter (4 September 1997–18 December 1997) ranged between 7.7 to 16.9, or an average of 10.2. For a prime-time audience discussion show, and especially one that was competing with so many other programs on newly arrived channels offering comedy, drama, and spectacle, this was remarkable. Flemings clearly wanted to see and hear other Flemings talk.

The Aesthetic of *Jan Publiek*

The set of *Jan Publiek* was basically round, a small amphitheatre divided into three seating areas and a proscenium. The panelists, expert guests, celebrity guests, and studio audience were arrayed in these seats, the twenty "unknown Flemings" mainly occupying the center section. Front and center, facing the panelists, was the host, who stood behind a podium. Most of the floor, part of the walls, the podium, and the borders around the seating area felt emotionally warm, constructed as they were of stained wood. The décor was largely geometric, in colors that were deep and complementary, whether the property of the set itself or of the lighting. In the middle of the proscenium was a round inlay, maize-colored, decorated in some abstract patterns but most prominently with a large black arrow that started at the host's podium and "aimed" at the panelists.

Behind the podium and to either side was a thick royal blue bar of light—not too bright—framing the host. He stood before a jumbo screen that sometimes projected the title *Jan Publiek* in black over a mottled maize background (black and yellow being the colors of the Flemish flag). At other times, the screen projected prefilmed segments of the program. Another screen was available beyond the blue bar to the host's left to project still headshots of the twenty panelists. At the back of the set, down one of the aisles between two of the seating sections, was a tunnel through which the host entered at the beginning of the show. Also in the back, high up on a "wall," was a large clock that told real time, signifying that *Jan Publiek* was broadcast live. A camera on a boom zoomed in on it near the show's end. This simple, formal yet warm and modern set was completed by the carefully, sometimes formally, dressed panelists and the show's guests, who numbered perhaps sixty altogether. The host, too, was formally attired, often in a three-piece suit. Whatever else this program would be, it began in a tasteful and dignified fashion.

The liveliness of *Jan Publiek* had to occur in spite of some obstacles. There were many panelists and guests, so many that when the camera pulled back to depict them all, they were faces in a crowd—the "publiek" that the show intended to capture and represent to the home audience. The many panelists and guests and the host were fixed in their positions, whether sitting (panel-ists) or standing (host). They could gesture, but that was about all. It was the technology that provided the movement: five cameras on wheels or booms varied the shot height, angle, and distance; occasionally a camera actually moved in on a speaker in a rather dramatic fashion. But by and large, these were talking heads. The screens offered extra-set visuals and gave a sense of intimacy to the whole environment, as though Van Rompaey, the panelists, and the home audience were watching television together (Van Rompaey swiveled around to view the screen behind him as the prefilmed segments were played). The timing for this movement, as for the whole live show, was impeccable.

Both the timing and the technological prowess of the show were on dis-play in the opening. When television viewers tuned into *Jan Publiek*, here is what we saw. The television screen became a computer monitor, on which we followed a cursor clicking on a *Jan Publiek* website at a pace that was in synch with the perky electronic theme music. The cursor selected window after window, resulting in a cascade that depicted Jan Van Rompaey's career on VRT from *Echo* forward, offering clips of him as a young man and moving chronologically forward. The cursor clicked on various scenes of Flanders and Belgium, including bicycle races and the Belgian king greeting his sub-jects. The music was vaguely pop-folk, with a chorus singing, not lyrics, but a refrain of "oh oh-oh oh-oh oh-ooooh" that climbed up the scale by half-steps. The prominent bass and the kettle drums beat at the pace of a brisk walk, purposeful, slightly quickening. One of the scenes on the computer monitor superimposed in cursive Flemish script the word "Yours." Another showed the cursor making selections among icons labeled with various emotions:

joy, despair, anger. The transition from the prefilmed segment to the live scene was dramatically realized by a camera on a boom that started high and followed Jan Van Rompaey striding forth from under the tunnel and past the panelists to assume his place behind the podium.

Four Panelists Through Their Speech Genres

When Sonja Spee and I began to contemplate together the accomplishment that was *Jan Publiek*, we wondered whether, despite the producers' elaborate attempts at fairness and egalitarianism, some panelists might have spoken more than others. Van Rompaey was ever mindful of giving the panelists equal time. Indeed, this was one of the reasons that panelists were frustrated by the brevity of their individual interventions (the point made by Carpentier). Spee and I discovered that we were right, that some panelists did speak more than others. One of the three who spoke the most also had the advantage of appearing in a prefilmed segment during the final episode of the show, singled out, as she was, as the oldest member of the panel. My hypothesis was that Van Rompaey might call on some panelists more often than others (if only unconsciously) because they were in some way better speakers. Spee had already been involved in a research project that yielded quantitative measurements of *Jan Publiek* speakers, but I was interested in determining qualitatively how people spoke. The primary methodology was the analysis of the speech genre (Dixon). In the end, I was hopeful that we might have some idea why some panelists spoke more than others, but also in general how panelists shaped their television persona over the sixteen episodes.

In this chapter, I am rereading the study (Dixon and Spee) in light of the thesis of this book. Talk shows contribute to democratic politics by means of the art of rhetoric, where "art" refers to craft, but also to aesthetics. The investigation becomes not just how did people talk so that they could claim the floor longer on a talk show like *Jan Publiek*, but how did they make themselves and their views known, make art, make connections to other people via the medium of this television talk show, *Jan Publiek*? How did their politics—their beliefs, their orientation to the world and to their fellows—intersect with their art—their creativity, their sense of beauty, decorum, and play?

The final episode of the first season of *Jan Publiek* was a retrospective. In addition to prefilmed segments that took us behind the scenes and into the lives of two panelists, Van Rompaey also announced the results of audience opinion surveys about the show. These gave us an idea of how the panelists were received by the home viewers, after the twenty "unknown Flemings" became "known unknown Flemings." The final episode made it clear that the audience had in fact created a narrative out of the season, and in the process had made "characters" out of the panelists. Spee and I followed their lead, in a sense, as we, too, created characters out of Betty, Rudi, Damien, and Simone. Two of them, Betty and Rudi, spoke more than other panelists, as did Simone—in her case, partly by virtue of being singled out in the final episode. Damien, however, spoke less. We included him to help us determine why panelists did and did not get chosen to speak. In this chapter, these characters are largely reinterpreted to gain a greater appreciation for the artistry of each.

On the show, the host and the producers attempted to make each of these "characters" fit within the larger *Jan Publiek* ethic and aesthetic. Even more than most talk shows, this one was highly dialogic and egalitarian, yet the dialogue was often bent toward the light, genial satire of the host, who generally controlled the flow of talk. He tried gamely to give everyone a chance to speak, and to have every perspective heard. This is consistent with the larger speech genre of the audience discussion program. In the case of *Jan Publiek*, it was a hybrid of the masculine public debate show *Het Lagerhuis* from Holland (one can see this in Van Rompaey's own demeanor and his placement behind a podium), the feminine afternoon talk show from the United States (*Jan Publiek*'s typical topics, like dieting, and its emphasis on feelings and opinions), and a number of other borrowings (including the man-on-the-street genre at which Van Rompaey excels). The panelists themselves had their own sense of artistry and ethics, which either blended or contended with the dominant ones shaped by the host and producers. Because of the format of the show, it was their short speeches and the back-and-forth banter with Van Rompaey that primarily communicated these ends. The speech genres themselves were small works of creativity that carried or miscarried in the environment of *Jan Publiek* according to how well formed they were, and how well suited they were to the interactive moment, and to the overall design of the show.

Comrade Betty: Didactic Speechifying

Betty was a definite standout. In her mid-thirties, she was fashionable in a Spartan way. Her wheat blonde hair was close-cropped, giving her face a broad, open quality. She was attired simply, conservatively. She sat erect, poised, as though on the edge of her chair, ready to perform. Her expression was generally serious. Although she often spoke in response to the talk of her fellow panelists, she had very little informal interaction with them. Already during the selection process she made it clear to the program makers that she supported the women's movement, that she was a member of the Socialist Party and a trade unionist. She indicated to the producers that she wanted to express her own personal and political opinions in public. A schoolteacher with the city of Antwerp, known for its leftist educational policies, Betty often identified herself in this way on the show.

She requested the floor frequently, got it more often than her colleagues, and held it by virtue of her excellent speechmaking abilities. Betty brought to *Jan Publiek* a town hall idiom, and her speech genre most typically was that of an impromptu political speech or mini-lecture. In the episode on "Migrant Riots" Betty got the floor after a highly animated discussion between two panel members who were trading heated comments back and forth. The opening speech act is an announcement of her identity:

> Betty: Well, I'm a teacher in vocational training and we organize training practice, and this is not the first time that the place for the teaching practice cancels the minute they hear there are immigrants youths involved.
>
> Van Rompaey: Some kind of discrimination. . . .
>
> Betty: And what concerns me the most is that with the young people here, they're now in Belgium and they stay here. In a couple of years they will be one of the foundations of our society and if we won't do anything to make that foundation as solid as possible, the system will collapse and we, Belgian people, are cooperating [in this] as well. And I think that's terrible! [Some members of the studio audience clap] (13 November 1997)

This speech, typical of Betty's oeuvre, is a little marvel of didactic rhetoric. It opens with a well-chosen example to illustrate in miniature the problem as Betty saw it. She moves along, reasoning through the topic of cause and effect, and winds up with a passionate denunciation that is implicitly a call to action. It is clear, concise, and easily understood by all. To accomplish all this and to move along as quickly as she does is not an easy task. Her delivery is acute, as well. She enunciates her words clearly and maintains a rhythm that matched the urgency of her meaning. The final sentence is both an exclamation—and delivered as such—and an emotional mooring for the whole speech. Betty's ethos comports perfectly with the speech itself: serious, earnest, intelligent, knowledgeable, sincere—and she looks into the camera.

In a formal sense, this speech enacted a dialogue with the *Jan Publiek* aesthetic. In its parts, it is well formed (a beginning, middle, and end) and balanced (cause and effect). It sets up expectations that it fulfills. Although passionate, it did not break the bounds of decorum. Even further, in its content, it reconfirms the founding communal ideal of *Jan Publiek*. The speech evidenced a respect for the audience; it offered its corrective vision in a mode of civility. It is dialogic in another way too—Betty performed properly for the host and the producers of the show. She met sound-bite requirements in the brevity of the speech but also in its piquancy. The speech would hold the audience's attention. Betty, then, had a talent for speaking under the unusually tight restrictions of television talk, and, especially, talk on Jan Publiek, which elevated the principle of equal access for its twenty regular panelists and guest experts very highly. Furthermore, because Betty pretty well always spoke like this, she was a dependable partner for host Jan Van Rompaey.

Betty's political commitments themselves dovetailed with some of those represented by Jan Publiek. It was, after all, the political left, specifically the feminist movement, that argued for the value of the personal in the public sphere. While Betty seemed as though she could easily mount the masculine podium behind which Van Rompaey stood, she also began and ended her speech with personal positioning, first making use of experience to claim an expertise, and, at the end, expressing her personal feelings on a subject that she had, to that point, rather carefully and rationally developed. Some of her language, especially in its personal and passionate declarations, fit well within the genre of the afternoon talk show that Jan Publiek imitated in part. However, on a number of occasions, she sidestepped Van Rompaey's invitations to provide the merely personal. Indeed, her interactions were noteworthy in their extreme didactic focus: Betty tended not to make jokes with Van Rompaey or asides to other panelists.

However, the moral earnestness that was at the heart of Betty's politics and aesthetics was ripe for the satiric plucking—thus, Comrade Betty. The Jan Publiek website made dialogic rejoinder to Betty's own announcements of identity, replete with wry commentary: "Betty werkt als leerkracht (en dat zullen we geweten hebben)"—"Betty works as a schoolteacher (and that we would have known)." And, frequently enough, when Betty began a speech by positioning herself, the host interrupted with "Yes, we know, go on, go on." The figure of the schoolteacher is in contemporary times gendered feminine and thereby made diminutive in intellectual stature (see Susan Miller). In terms of class, the schoolteacher is the moral guardian of bourgeois values, keeping the roving proles and errant bourgies in line—at least while they're in the classroom.

By poking fun at Betty, Van Rompaey and the producers were reintegrating her into the light aesthetic and dialogic communalism that was Jan Publiek. She was a standout, sure, but a funny one, maybe even a likeable, quirky one, because her persona was crafted in dialogue with the host and producers of the show. Betty may have blazed with political commitment, but *Jan Publiek* brought her down to earth. Betty fit neatly into *Jan Publiek's* overall plan. She was, in fact, someone with the "striking personality" that the producers of *Jan Publiek* were looking for, of the "type" of the liberated woman, philosophical orator, a person of sharp opinions.

Betty's political aesthetic in some ways seemed a throwback to pre-televisual modernity, McLuhan's "hot" speechmaker (too much informa-tion)—another reason that it was easy for Van Rompaey to satirize her. But she was well suited to a new kind of melodrama into which *Jan Publiek* would stumble, rather ominously, in the "Migrant Riots" episode, discussed in the last section of this chapter.

Rudi: The Populist Aesthetic of the New Mediated Man

To learn about the *Jan Publiek* panelists, one might have viewed the show's website. Rudi, however, had his own website. He was a businessman who marketed forty gardening centers, but he also marketed himself. Both the *Jan Publiek* website and his own promoted his two books on entrepreneurism: *Onmogelijk bestaat niet* (The Impossible Does Not Exist) and *Omdat het anders moet* (Because Things Should Change). These commercial speech genres and speech acts carried the illocutionary force of "buy this!," as did, in a different way, Rudi's invitation to discover "the man behind the public figure." Before there was talk of personal branding, Rudi already understood it. Before reality television, Rudi was practicing the cultivation of his own celebrity. He did this so skillfully that in the last segment of *Jan Publiek*, Van Rompaey com-mented about audience response to Rudi: "Rudi, people thought you were sympathetic, a handsome man."

The audience responded well to Rudi because he was so personable. Like Betty, Rudi could speak and carry himself in both masculine and feminine ways, but, unlike Betty, whose speeches drew attention to themselves, Rudi drew attention to himself—and to his relation to others. Betty's preferred speech genre was the speech or lecture; Rudi had several—the confession, the conversation, the promotion. He was (as already advertised!) handsome and well dressed in a relaxed way, a man who exhibited a certain charisma and easy authority. Central to his self-promoting ethos, though, was some-thing downright lovable, maybe even cuddly.

One such lovable quality was his proclivity for self-revelation. Rudi man-aged the confession speech genre in expert fashion. In 1997, this genre would be stratified as youthful and/or feminine, but Rudi was far from unmanned by it. During the episode on "Children, a Blessing?" (2 October 1997), Rudi outed himself as a gay man. The older, conventionally masculine Jan Van Rompaey was taken aback by the admission, but Rudi responded with what

Austin might call a verdictive, a pronouncement made by someone with great authority. "This," he decreed, "cannot be such an important revelation," and carried on in his easy, conversational genre. Van Rompaey greeted the confession genre with satire, but for Rudi it seemed to be second nature. He easily deflected Van Rompaey's attempts at "fencing" with bland literality. In the "Dieting" (16 October 1997) episode, Van Rompaey asked if the panelists if they thought that they could lose weight through their own willpower.

> Rudi: Yes, I er . . . at a certain moment I thought that I was too fat and I started a diet, called Montignac. I can strongly recommend it to everyone, I did suggest it earlier this week to Kristel [one of the celebrities who was on the show] . . .
>
> Van Rompaey: So, your Body Mass Index is a bit too high?
>
> Rudi: Yes, er, I'll have to diet again. I have eaten cakes today, so . . .

Here, the confession ("I was too fat"; "I have eaten cakes today") exists in dialogic relation with the commercial testimonial ("I can strongly recommend the diet to everyone") that is simultaneously a friendly self-promotion, as Rudi made himself the equivalent of a celebrity ("I did suggest it earlier this week to Kristel")—although the latter speech act takes the form of an expositive: Rudi was merely informing us of an accomplished fact. We saw that Van Rompaey might be described as an aristocratic democrat; we see in Rudi the new figure of the populist who makes himself one of the crowd (Rudi, too, has weight problems), yet also stands above it in the glimmering world of celebrity.

Rudi both extended and bent the *Jan Publiek* ethic and aesthetic. Although self-promoting, he also reached out to others. Many women as well as men could relate to his confession that after he lost more than thirteen kilos of weight, he started eating French—and Belgian!—fries again. He concluded by saying:

> But it gives you a pleasurable feeling and I think it's up to you. I think that Damien goes too hard at it. I think that when you arrive at a certain moment in your life, that you stand in front of your mirror and you say to yourself: I'm not looking so good anymore. But yes, everyone has to decide for himself or herself. (16 October 1997)

This last phrase is a cliché of democracy, and again, blandly offered. Van Rompaey might have made a career out of listening to "the man on the street," but Rudi sounded as though he was one of them. Notably nonsexist in his language (an advance beyond even the title of "Jan Publiek"), his new style of masculine authority made use of (formerly) feminine speech genres worked through commercial and mass-mediated forms. The Flemish public are transforming from aggrieved subjects demanding rights into the consumers in the "global village" that McLuhan described. There, people prefer to relate rather than debate. Rudi's performance on *Jan Publiek* seems representative of this new development.

Significantly, Rudi directed some of his speech acts to fellow panelists. Sitting next to the elderly Simone, gesturing toward her, touching her, he said that she was "like a mother to me now." This provoked a sly rejoinder from the more traditionally masculine Van Rompaey: "Maybe you need one, a mother like her, right now." Van Rompaey was no doubt parodying a genre from pop psychology, but Rudi, not an ironic man, was completely unfazed. "I sure do," he replied. To judge by other speech acts addressed to him, it appears that he had indeed achieved one of the perlocutionary effects he sought: the audience admired him, Simone returned his affections, and he himself claimed that his biggest gain in being on the show was that "I've made a lot of friends." That he censured Damien for making fun of dieting can only go in his favor; dieting was, of course, chosen as a topic for *Jan Publiek* because of its popularity, and Damien himself turned out to be not so very popular. Rudi was a most media-savvy "ordinary person," a man exhibiting a postmodern *sprezzatura*. He actually succeeded in providing an alternative definition of *Jan Publiek*, one that was not distanced and satiric, but, in the McLuhan formulation, "participatory." Rudi seemed in control of a new political aesthetic that essentially trumped Van Rompaey's.

Damien: The Old Orality Meets the New

Where Rudi worked easily within the confines of *Jan Publiek* (and the medium of television) to suit his own purposes, Damien's objective—to "step on tender toes"—made his performance on the show more difficult. By the end of the season, the audience deemed him "a bitter man," and he himself expressed regret and dissatisfaction with the whole process of the show. He said he felt the five cameras of *Jan Publiek* bearing down on him. Van Rompaey himself seemed to go beyond a genial satire in his some of his interactions with Damien. If anyone's toes were stepped on, they would seem to have been Damien's. Over the course of the entire season, Damien spoke less than Betty, Rudi, or Simone, but in this chapter, his case gets more space proportionately, since I will expend special effort to determine what it was about his aesthetic, his values, and his interactive style that so clashed with those of *Jan Publiek*.

The camera was not especially kind to Damien. His face was long and somewhat pointed at chin and nose, he wore eyeglasses with a glittery chain that looped to the back of his neck, and he dressed in sweaters that looked slightly lumpy. He was not always clear in his communications. He certainly did attempt to stir up trouble on *Jan Publiek*, but he did not try to rouse his fellows to combat; he only carried on an odd, isolated, yet ultimately rather mild campaign apparently aimed at showing up some of the pretensions of *Jan Publiek*. None of the data collected by VRT or by any of three researchers of the *Jan Publiek* makes Damien's class clear, but perhaps, like Betty, Damien was chosen to be a type of "striking personality" meant to draw audience attention. He did not speak as much as our other three panelists, but it was true that when he did, he stood out.

However we might categorize Damien's performance, we can certainly see that it was oppositional to the world of *Jan Publiek* as created not only by the host and producers, but by the other panelists and home audience too—although any of these constituencies may well have taken some delight in scowling at Damien. But if Damien had wanted to be in control, to be an apt jester of official discourse, he would have needed a different performance. Such a performance would have required a different aesthetic: a lightness of foot, an ability to engage with the opponent by using the opponent's own weight against him, a perfect sense of timing, and a flair for the dramatic. These Damien did not have—at least not onstage, not on camera. Nonetheless, Damien succeeded occasionally in calling attention to the "polite society" side of *Jan Publiek*. Ultimately, it appears that Damien himself was unsatisfied with his performance on the show. By the end of the season he seemed forced to inhabit a character he did not choose, forged in part by the dynamic interplay between him and the other players on the show, especially the host.

We can see Damien flouting the rules of polite society during an episode on prostitution (20 November 1997), featuring a woman advocate for prostitutes' rights. *Jan Publiek* host and panelists carefully comported themselves, treating the guest with the middle-class respect due her as citizen activist. There were no embarrassing moments (and no other male panelists spoke) until Damien cut through with an off-color joke. The joke as speech genre was constant companion to Van Rompaey, but Van Rompaey himself would only skirt the risqué. Damien, however, joked that prostitutes could charge a value-added tax to their services since "a man goes in smaller than he comes out." The joke is stratified for an all-male or working-class gathering, perhaps a pub. There one may hear jokes aplenty that build upon human types (the mother, the whore, the stupid guy), many of which sharply etch lines of sex, gender, race, and ethnicity. McLuhan's protégé Walter Ong linked typological language of this kind to "orality," a way of being in the world that depends on oral communication as opposed to literate. Its defining genres are epics, fairy tales, riddles, and other highly memorable forms—in this case, the punchline joke. It is a genre in which the prostitute herself excels. She adroitly quips in reply: "No, that's wrong: the man comes out smaller." The illocutionary force of her speech act—"I win"—produces the effect that she implies (Damien *is* now "smaller"). Such direct but playful confrontation would create solidarity in a pub, but on *Jan Publiek* it worked against Damien, marking him as vulgar, rude, and—of course—sexist, which, in Flanders, where public speech is regulated by the state, borders on the illegal.

As might be expected, Damien's speech acts did not unite him with other panelists. Rudi did criticize him for making fun of dieting, but otherwise the panelists tended to ignore him. Sometimes his aims were so difficult to comprehend that others simply could not respond. An example comes from an episode called "The Law is the Law" (23 October 1997), where the host asked a hypothetical moral question: "In an American prison, where smoking is forbidden, a condemned man uttered his last wish which was to smoke one cigarette. What would you do, if you were the governor?"

Damien: I would not give it to him.

Van Rompaey: Why not?

Damien: Bad for his health.

Van Rompaey: Ha ha . . . okay, but besides that. It would have been a matter of no concern if he were still healthy or not.

Damien: If necessary two . . .

Van Rompaey: If necessary two. Er . . . Astrid? (23 October 1997)

Van Rompaey's man-on-the-street questioning, practiced over years of work on VRT television shows, met Damien's barroom parody of legal hairsplitting. Damien's speech act, "bad for his health," is a complicated rejoinder. It provides the punchline for the joke, the illocutionary force of which is: How ridiculous! Who cares? As well, the speech genre works as a rejoinder to Rudi's discourse on health and dieting. Although Van Rompaey himself had satirized Rudi's language, he now must labor to maintain the show's focus. Van Rompaey attempts to recast Damien's character as citizen, that is, someone who will give his sincere opinion on a matter of public concern, the law. Even given a second chance, Damien continues on his collision course with the host with a final rejoinder that falls flat ("if necessary two"), perplexing Van Rompaey. Damien's eccentric speech acts impaired Van Rompaey in his identity as host, surely a rather stressful position in a live program. This was probably one of the reasons Damien was called on less often than many other panelists.

In an earlier episode, Van Rompaey initiated an aggressive joke with Damien. The host and producers all had knowledge of each panelist's background, so it was probably not by chance that Van Rompaey decided to interview Damien about his large family. The speech genre is that of the vaudeville routine, with Damien as the unwitting, or at least unwilling, partner. Damien's tendency to offer small bullets of dialogue added to the humor.

Van Rompaey: Damien . . . was born in a family of, er, how many was it?

Damien: Fourteen.

Van Rompaey: Excuse me?

Damien: Fourteen.

Van Rompaey: Fourteen children—

Damien: —and I'm the only son.

Van Rompaey: Yeah, so thirteen sisters.

Damien: Which means I have thirteen fantastic sisters.

Van Rompaey: Was it bearable?

Damien: Oh yeah, it was.

Van Rompaey: Yeah, well . . . was it always . . . yeah, well . . . like a big family . . . er, were they like always together?

Damien: No, not very often. Most of us were placed in boarding schools, but er, we still managed to be a solid crew.

Damien did not "play along" willingly, even though this genre could easily be within his repertoire. He instead took on the role of protective brother, as though shielding his family from criticism. The studio of *Jan Publiek* was not a second home to him, as it seemed to be to Rudi (who, we recall, shrugged off Van Rompaey's attempt to make Rudi's homosexuality an exceptional thing). If Damien wished to offer a critique to *Jan Publiek*, it was from outside, and perhaps below, from an inferior position.

Van Rompaey then switched to another speech genre, the therapeutic interview—a staple of the afternoon talk show—but here probably reaccented as a joke. The hyperbolic term *traumatized* suggests satire again. But Damien took the question literally—as though he were traumatized by Van Rompaey!—and tried to move away from it as quickly as possible.

Van Rompaey: Has it traumatized you?

Damien: No, not traumatized. What I've missed is a brother, but hey, it was the way it was.

Van Rompaey: Yes.

Damien: I've had to be satisfied with thirteen sisters.

Van Rompaey: Yes.

Damien: But thirteen beauties, and they still are.

Van Rompaey: Yes, well I'm sure they're all watching tonight.

Damien: I hope so, yeah. [He laughs] (2 October 1997)

It may be that Damien tried to situate Van Rompaey as a gallant man when Damien pronounced his sisters to be "thirteen beauties." Most of Damien's and Van Rompaey's utterances were stratified differently, as though they were playing different games. That is probably the case here, too, at the end of this dialogue. But gentlemen do exist within both of these worldviews, and it was one of the few instances of agreement between the two.

In reflecting upon the above interactions, it is all too clear how one man's aesthetic is another man's pain. One is reminded of Propp's analysis of the folktale when Damien describes his sisters as "thirteen beauties"; or when he refers to a man as a "henpecked husband"; or, in the episode on nakedness (11 September 1997), refers to his own "crown jewels" as succinct evidence for why he will not go naked in public. There is a truth and loveliness to seeing people in their mythic register that Van Rompaey's light and sparkling satire, individuated as it is, could not allow. Or perhaps, better put, it might have been well for the mythic and the ironic to have been brought together here, in whatever way it could have been done. For this theme will reappear in the "Migrant Riots" episode, and still later in Belgian and Flemish politics, as Enlightenment Europe comes into conflict with conservative Islam, individuation into conflict with traditionalism. Here, Damien seemed to lack the capacity for effectual oppositional talk on *Jan Publiek*, but whether this was due to a lack of rhetorical talent—an adaptive talent, surely, and he was not adapting to the requirements of talk on *Jan Publiek*—or to Damien's position as a working-class man with traditional values, or simply to Damien's prickly personality was not clear. It does seem as though *Jan Publiek* defined politics and aesthetics such that Damien did not appear to be a highly valued part of the "public."

During the last segment of the show, the host confronted Damien with audience members' description of him as "a bitter man; he seems to be a bitter man." This time, Damien could not even muster his usual truncated verbal response; he offered only a tight defensive smile. When Van Rompaey made the question a direct one—"Are you a bitter man?"—Damien nodded and waved Van Rompaey off, but the host pressed on. Damien had to say twice after that, "No more questions," as though releasing himself from the witness stand. This was one of the few moments on *Jan Publiek* where one can get the squeamish feeling that reality shows can provide—that "defining moment of revelation" that Rachel Moseley writes about regarding "makeover" television programs (301). But *Jan Publiek* was not a reality television show; it was an audience discussion show in which the panelists' views and intentions were supposed to matter—they were not to be merely fodder for the spectacle. Damien had become a type, the "bitter man." On the light and upbeat *Jan Publiek*, that made him virtually a villain. The transformation of Damien's image was accomplished via television, a conveyor of Walter Ong's "secondary orality"—the predominant communicative "technology" of our own time, partly built on the literate mode, partly circling back to the old oral one. Secondary orality may play again with human types, but differently: a new "type" may be minted in a moment. One must be aware of how the political aesthetic is shaping around one minute by minute. No better statement could be made to emphasize the respect that one must have for the power of television, a power that is not only technological and economic, but social and performative.

Simone: Playing the Woman

At seventy-two, Simone was the oldest of the panelists of *Jan Publiek*. She was an ample and sturdy woman whose hair was always carefully styled and who generally wore a loose-fitting dress, often a floral print. Simone was a pensioner at the time, but had been an owner of, and waitress in, a café in Antwerp. She was a longtime admirer of Jan Van Rompaey, and from the outset had intentions of claiming his attentions in order to turn a media eye onto problems faced by the elderly. In her elder years, Simone had become something of an advocate. Her speech on *Jan Publiek* ranged widely, in ways that intersected with, but also differed from, Rudi's. Like Betty, Simone took up the banner of citizen; like Damien, she brought a more traditional aesthetic to the show; like Rudi, she was friendly and engaging with the host. One of Simone's talents as a rhetorician was to know which genre to use and when to create the relationships she wished to make.

One of the most charming moments on *Jan Publiek* occured in a prerecorded segment aired on the final episode. In documentary fashion, we followed Simone around Antwerp. The illocutionary force of this speech act was to apotheosize the Simone into celebrity. She handled the role competently, but pleased and surprised as though she'd suddenly awakened and found herself the queen mother on parade. She graciously accepted questions from admirers on the street; "I've seen you on *Jan Publiek*," one gushed. In the pharmacy she exchanged important information on prescriptions with a fellow customer. Finally, at the Senior Center we were among Simone's friends, who joked and mugged for the camera; a heavily mascaraed woman winked at the man behind it, salaciously, humorously. An interviewer queried as to whether they all feel Simone has changed over the three months on *Jan Publiek*, but they were hopelessly lost to another agenda, parodying themselves (and perhaps their former identities), teasing the bustling youth, us prurient viewers. They were putting us on. In this episode of *Jan Publiek*, the final one of the season, we were treated to something rarely seen on television: a present mode lavishly and lovingly satirized by one from the past. If Simone had achieved nothing else, this alone would be noteworthy.

It was not exactly what she said she had sought, which was to bring attention to the elderly as victims of neglect. Briefly on air and apparently in letters that she had written to Van Rompaey, she partook of the speech genre of the complaint, which is often, and in many cultures, stratified as an elderly woman's genre. Traditionally, elderly woman are expected to have complaints and to air them, particularly to their children. In the proper order of things, children are thought to owe something to their mother, who has sacrificed for them. This is a genre that predates by far the television talk show, yet there would seem to be some carryover into the language of the weeping victims often depicted on afternoon talk shows. But Simone maintained a posture of dignity, and addressed the younger and male Van Rompaey not as confessor or revealer of inner secrets, but as a man with the power to help set things aright.

Selected as a panelist on *Jan Publiek*, Simone began to write letters to Van Rompaey, voicing complaints about the show and about the ghettoizing of old people, about their loneliness, and about her own inability to reach around and wash her back while bathing. On these matters she had been writing to newspapers for years, well before *Jan Publiek*. Simone was born into an era of letter writing, to a class of women who wrote regularly of family news, history, and gossip. Still, she seemed a "natural" on *Jan Publiek*. How could this woman who came of age before the birth of television make such good use of it? One answer is that, like Rudi, who was her "friend," Simone was socially adept.

Simone was particularly skilled at interacting well with the host. On the live portion of that final episode, Simone sounded "the complaint" and invoked Van Rompaey as son—she noted with some asperity that she had been writing him. The host neatly deflected the criticism (he had not replied to her letters) by turning attention back to her and her feelings: "and you wrote that something bothered you." Yes, she replied, the panelists should have had more time to speak their minds—in particular, she had wanted to take up the cause of the elderly. On another occasion, during the prostitute episode, we saw the host's courtly attitude toward Simone. She began her turn by referring to herself: "when I was still young and beautiful," to which Van Rompaey replied:

Van Rompaey: Yes, you're still beautiful, Simone. If you—

Simone: Oh yeah, ha ha!

Van Rompaey: —allow me to say that. (18 December 1997)

Never replying to her letters, Van Rompaey nonetheless did repay her attentions. In general (and not just with Van Rompaey), Simone seemed well liked. We recall that Rudi regarded her as a mother. Also, the audience and host commented favorably on her propensity for good-natured joking.

As her café work might suggest, Simone seemed to have built a longstanding identity as hostess (20 November 1997). She was introduced at the beginning of the prostitution episode because she lived near the red light district (the Zakstraat), a working- to lower-class area. When queried about that, Simone did not take offense, but embarked on a joke.

Simone: Yes, yes the Zakstraat, because er, I used to own a café and one day there were some Dutch people and, um, my place was full, and one of them said they wanted a seat by the window, and I said, "Yes, but then you have to go to the Zakstraat."

Van Rompaey: Yes, there you have a lot of people by the window [where prostitutes advertise their wares]. [Audience and panel members laugh] (20 November 1997)

We note that while Simone's joke roughly corresponds to the genre used by Damien on the prostitute episode—it skirts the risqué, it is homely—it is not crude or direct (Damien's joke comes down with a thwack), nor is it competitive. Simone's ready deployment of joking and bantering as speech genres made her a dependable dialogic partner for Van Rompaey—the cheerfully bantering hostess to his host—and he called on her with obvious confidence and pleasure.

Simone conformed to the light and genial aesthetic of *Jan Publiek* while still bringing something different to it. In attempting to achieve her personal and political ends, Simone performed roles that often seem as typological as those suggested by Damien's language. Certainly his and her political aesthetics with regard to gender seemed to agree. Yet she deployed them differently, and for a different end. She used them to build relationships, especially with the host, but also with the panelists and the audience—with all for whom *Jan Publiek* was a genre to be collectively fulfilled. In her roles as hostess and grande dame she laid a foundation of levity; in her grandmother complainant role, she established gravity. In all, she parlayed to her advantage the authority traditionally accorded old women. She could count on Van Rompaey, with whose public persona she was well acquainted, to dance the appropriate *pas de deux*. Simone's hostess and grande dame might befit a "star of stage and screen," but because the television as medium can "quote" from all past visual media—"[t]elevision was hypermediated even before the advent of digital graphics" (Bolter and Grusin 185)—Simone's performance can be received in the new surround of this medium, this television genre, this *Jan Publiek*. Simone's notion of citizen advocacy overlapped slightly with Betty's—both argued for rights for groups of people, not just for their own personal gain—but the political aesthetic differed greatly. Like Rudi's it was populist and relational, but, unlike his, it was more heavily stylized and typologized. Simone's performance had surprising range within the constraints that are both self-imposed and imposed by history and culture.

A Summary

In many ways, the Habermasian notion of public sphere did not well suit *Jan Publiek*, and perhaps not any audience discussion show, since most of them, like television in general, exist to entertain. However, something of the ethos that created the notion of public sphere also subtends *Jan Publiek*. From the title of the program to the desire to represent Flemings accurately among the panelists to the attempt to give all panelists equal time to speak, *Jan Publiek* did contribute to a televisual "public sphere." Nancy Fraser explains in a general way why it is that public spheres that are nominally democratic actually are not:

> Historians such as Joan Landes (1988), Geoff Eley (1991), Mary Ryan (1990, 1991), and Evelyn Brooks-Higginbotham (1993) have shown that discursive interaction within official bourgeois public spheres has consistently been governed by protocols of style and decorum that were also markers of status inequality. These protocols functioned *informally* to marginalize women, plebeians, and members of subordinate racialized groups, preventing them from participating as peers *even after their formal incorporation*. (1995, 289)

Fraser borrows here from Bourdieu's critique of middle-class aesthetics when she mentions "protocols of style and decorum" as factors that exclude people from the public sphere. But the list of people so excluded ("women, plebeians, and members of subordinate racialized groups") each have different relations to middle-class aesthetics. That was seen quite clearly on *Jan Publiek* by looking closely at the performances of our four panelists. Just to consider class identity itself (as best we can determine, since *Jan Publiek* did not overtly consider class), we can see that Simone shone while Damien sputtered, and that Betty's decidedly middle-class schoolteacher persona drew satirical criticism. It will not do to indict aesthetics itself, as though only the bourgeois class has it, because what may be happening is a clash of aesthetics, a clash inflected by more than just class. Bakhtin's dialogism is crucial to our understanding here. The various rhetorics that were being practiced on *Jan Publiek* came together for negotiation, compromise, and conflict.

Jan Publiek did have an overall aesthetic of balance and a light formality that actually did enable a wide range of performances by its panelists. Through dialogue with the host and with the other panelists, each panelist was certainly invited to broach the negotiation. But its broad goal of egalitarianism can only ever be an ideal. Not only were some people better speakers or performers than others, and therefore better able to claim more time on camera, different rhetorics themselves were better suited to the aesthetic of *Jan Publiek*.

Betty's didacticism was too uppity for the populist demands of television generally and of *Jan Publiek* specifically, but Jan Van Rompaey's gentle irony could rein her in. Her skillfulness in her chosen form of rhetoric, the mini-speech or lecture, was strong; she provided the host with a known quantity and with something of the seriousness and focus that the show's very premise required. The show needed a dialogue with a well-spoken, thoughtful person. That Betty did not contest her satiric portrait but instead kept to her didactic character made her a comfortable resident of *Jan Publiek*. Betty's leftist politics and aesthetics were conformable to *Jan Publiek*. Damien's oppositional ones provided a more complex problem that proved insuperable. The rather ungallant prosecution of Damien in the concluding episode was not only injurious to Damien, but to the balance of *Jan Publiek*. Of course, putting Damien on the spot did serve the interests of entertainment—something perhaps required by the "Jan Publiek" of the home audience. For his own stated purposes, Damien either chose the wrong speech genres or could not execute them properly under the conditions of *Jan Publiek*. His predicament suggests that it might take a formidably talented person to carry out a masculine, working-class critique (if that was what it is) of *Jan Publiek*. For practical reasons, this live show could not withstand direct challenges to the host; the whole edifice could have come tumbling down in real time.

That might be what some leftists would want. Presumably, though, some replacement edifice would have to be chosen. Maybe roomier, more durable, but it would still be shaped, artfully created. Is there a revolutionary aesthetics—on television, or anywhere else—that can include everyone? Could there ever be?

The closest currently on offer looks to be a populist aesthetic without *Jan Publiek*'s "classy" irony. Rudi provided some insight into that. The real revolutionaries, of late—the transformers of society—have been capitalists. Rudi's rhetorical performance moved adroitly across media, from books to websites to television as a means of publicity, uttered in genres that served his purposes admirably. The synergy carried over to the relationships he forged with the host and other panelists, and—through them—with the audience, his ultimate dialogic object. Betty may have believed she was speaking for the people, but Rudi was of the people. He declared directly that "everyone must decide for himself or herself." He was "of the people," he expressed belief in their capacity to choose wisely, he seemed to like them (he was friendly with other panelists—and also celebrities), and he shared their problems (e.g., needing to diet, trying to better himself through his business ventures), even if he was different from most of them (he was gay; he was a self-declared "public figure"); he criticized only the criticizers (like Damien). Rudi was also a skillful speaker, artfully employing the language of mass media (e.g., the infomercial testimonial), which everybody knows and can "relate to"; by this means, he was elevated. Unlike Damien, his speech acts furthered the smooth running of the show. Like Damien, Rudi issued a kind of challenge to Van Rompaey, but not through face-on confrontation. Rather, Rudi simply offered an alternative version of masculinity, one that can accede to its own superiority both by fiat and by populist identification. Like many successful television personalities and celebrities of this postmodern period (we are soon to visit one of them, Oprah Winfrey), Rudi was simultaneously above us and one of us.

All of the panelists of *Jan Publiek* became temporary celebrities—the twenty "unknown Flemish people" became the "well-known, unknown Flemish people"—but only a couple of them seemed able to parlay this opportunity into something memorable. Simone created through her well-chosen speech acts a persona that put her center stage as a good-natured hostess and dignified elder. Like Rudi, she wore her authority easily. Because of her good humor and because her persona centered on serving people, she was not in danger of appearing snooty when Simone the Celebrity graciously accepted the admiration of her subjects. Like Rudi, Simone was at once both above and below, and sought assiduously the opportunities open to the subordinate (e.g., she could challenge the male host without unmanning him—in contradistinction to Damien, perhaps).

The aesthetic on *Jan Publiek* was both populist and aristocratic, building on the millennia of struggles that contributed to a particular Western European style of civilization and representative democracy. Rudi's performance on the show seems to reflect the shift to another version of that Western European. It takes its authority from mass-mediated celebrity and capitalist ideology. This latest historical form is being challenged strongly by the recent group of Muslim immigrants to Belgium, whose own often-uncertain place in Belgium's capitalist enterprises and in her democratic institutions has literally and metaphorically changed the complexion of this small nation-state. As a sign of the times, *Jan Publiek* also reflected these changes.

The "Migrant Riots" Episode: An Aesthetic of Imbalance

Jan Publiek drew from the headlines for its discussion topics throughout the first season, although typically these were feature, not "hard news," headlines. The "Migrant Riots" episode (13 November 1997) brings to the show a hybridization between news commentary genres and political debate. But an underlying aesthetic works through melodrama. The aesthetics of melodrama contrasts sharply with an ideal of rational control that runs from the rhetorical theory of Aristotle to the journalistic theory that produces the hard news genre. Rationality, emotional restraint, classical balance, an emphasis on logos (knowledge, evidence) over pathos, and an ethos of the authoritative and trustworthy—all within the context of a largely secular worldview—these are ideal components of that aesthetic. Melodrama, by contrast, expresses an imbalance.

Melodrama grows out of a different worldview, one wherein control has been lost and no consolation found. Ben Singer sees melodrama as perhaps the signal genre of modernity, expressing in coded form the extremities of change and dislocation that people have experienced after the Industrial Revolution. He calls the narrative structure of melodrama "nonclassical," as it seems to defy the ordinary logic of cause and effect in its "preference for outrageous coincidence, implausibility" and so on (46). Singer (quoting Jacobs) argues that melodrama "tends to generate impasses in which the characters are trapped and find it difficult to take action, to make choices, or to move directly towards some goal" (43). Peter Brooks zeroes in on the quasi-religious nature of melodrama in its replacement of the moral clarity of organized religion by one of its own. Ethos is divided among extreme characters: victims, heroes, and villains. All of the above characteristics produce the wild swings of emotion and blatant spectacle that are melodrama's hallmarks.

The immigrant situation in Europe is complex. Certainly melodramatic terms—crisis, radical Islam, violence, and terror—are now associated with it. But however the analysis is done, it is clear that many European nationals and immigrants experience the impasses out of which melodrama is created. In the 1950s and 1960s "guest worker" programs were initiated in many European states to fill mostly unskilled positions on a presumably temporary basis. Nowadays, Europe sometimes also needs high-tech workers, partly because birthrates are decreasing. Immigrants are needed both to fill positions and to support pensioners. Muslim immigrants, largely from Turkey and northern Africa, have experienced dislocation and discrimination on a number of fronts (racial, religious, cultural, linguistic, and class background), as well as poverty—exactly the kind of experience of "modernity" that gives rise to melodrama, according to Singer (17–35). Europeans have a long history of attempting to maintain a strong sense of the national culture of their specific countries, making integration of immigrants more difficult: "European nations are not 'melting pots' of culture and naturalization of immigrants in European nations takes years, even generations" (Mukhopadhyay 110).

Simultaneously, European nationals have felt cornered by rising violence. The worst violence has occurred since *Jan Publiek* aired its "Migrant Riots" episode in the fall of 1997. Since then, some have been driven from melodrama and into silence:

> [M]ost disturbing is the fact that, apart from the indiscriminate killing of civilians in Madrid and London and the symbolic murder of Theo van Gogh, prominent European public figures have been facing death threats for their expressed views on Islam, Muslim societies in Europe and the role of women in Islam in the contemporary world. Ayaan Hirsi Ali, the Somalia-born Dutch Member of Parliament and coproducer of the controversial film *Submission* made by Theo van Gogh, and Mimount Bousakla, a socialist MP (of Moroccan origin) from Antwerp in Belgium, have both received threats and are under government protection . . . some columnists have decided to remain mute on contemporary issues [because] of a silent fear among resident Europeans, as well as in the Muslim intelligentsia, preventing them from expressing their viewpoints in public. (Mukhopadyay 105)

A European-Muslim scholar, Bassam Tibi, witnessed stern rebuke—in the form of "shouting"—when another colleague used the term "global jihad" (xv). That is indeed the kind of language that the *Telegraph* reports to be banned for use amongst government officials in the European Union: "Banned terms are said to include 'jihad,' 'Islamic' or 'fundamentalist.' . . . One alternative, suggested publicly last year, is for the term 'Islamic terrorism' to be replaced by 'terrorists who abusively invoke Islam'" (Waterfield). In Flanders, the right-wing Vlaams Belang party might be gaining support because it is willing to speak out in the name of a Flemish nationality (Dewinter). Moderate voices like Tibi are still managing to argue against Muslim colleagues that want "the Islamization of Europe" (xv). Against this latter aim, Tibi presents to his "fellow Muslim immigrants the alternative of a European Islam based on the values of civil society, to be shared by all who want to live in Europe as citizens of an open society" (xiv).

Tibi was writing in 2008. Some ten years earlier, judging by the "Migrant Riots" episode of *Jan Publiek*, an open society was thriving in Flanders. Panelists and guests were indeed eager to share their views. But that does not mean that *Jan Publiek*'s own standards of equality and accurate representation occurred. As in other episodes, Van Rompaey still strove to give everyone an equal airing. This time it cut short some important dialogues that might truly have shed some light on the conflicts. Another problem: owing to Belgium's policies of gathering population statistics, it is difficult to know the size of the Muslim immigrant population in Flanders at the time of *Jan Publiek*. What is clear is that only one out of twenty panelists in the first season—a woman named Fatiya—represented that community. Muslims who headed social welfare projects for immigrants or who were political activists were included as guests and explicitly invited to speak, as were ethnic Flemish policemen, journalists, politicians, and (the usual) celebrities. In addition, Van Rompaey called upon Fatiya more than usual, perhaps in an effort to even up the score, but also, almost certainly, because the discussion was short on logos with respect to the immigrant community. Fatiya turned out to be an excellent "informant," a term we borrow from anthropology, for Fatiya was doing more than offering her opinion—she was informing her fellow panelists, guests, host, and audience of a way of life that was apparently little known to them. Fatiya in this sense remained the "unknown Fleming" even by the end of the season.

Our interest will be not only in what was said in this discussion but in how it was said. The political aesthetic was no longer light and egalitarian. It was intense, dramatic, and partisan. The prefilmed sequences contributed to the melodrama, with an opening spectacle that cast the rioting youths as villains and then showed them to be inarticulate in later journalistic interviews. The show ended with an elderly Flemish woman, backlit so that her face was obscured, narrating a tale of terror in which (presumably) Muslim youths rampaged and ransacked the first floor of her home while she cowered upstairs. The melodramatic narrative of the show was episodic, often comprised of vignettes of verbal sparring that ended in triumph for one and defeat for another, or, if Van Rompaey intervened, in frustrating interruption. The overarching narrative began and ended in spectacle, with, we might say, a cliffhanger ending. When respite from this kind of intensity did occur on this show, it tended to be sentimental, a platitudinous "let's all live together"—another characteristic of melodrama, the sentimental ending. In Bakhtinian terms, the discussion was less dialogic and more monologic—a big problem, perhaps, for an audience discussion program. Our analysis will note two things especially. First was the undertow of melodrama, where rioting boys, policemen, and even *Jan Publiek* panelists were cast (or cast themselves or each other) as victims, victim-heroes, or villains. Second, we will examine closely the one instance where Fatiya tried to move fellow panelist Albert beyond melodrama and into an "internally persuasive" dialogic, as Bakhtin would term it.

On 13 November 1997, the topic for discussion on *Jan Publiek* was the immigrant riots in Anderlecht, a neighborhood of Brussels. It had displaced the previously announced topic of prostitution—"because of the urgency," according to Van Rompaey's introduction. The episode began with an extended journalistic footage of a mass protest march and, among some, rioting: young people overturning cars, breaking windows in the city hall, eluding the pursuing policemen. The precipitant for the march itself was the death of a young Moroccan named Said, shot by the police as he fled from them. He was presumed to be a drug dealer. The protest march was actually organized by Flemish Communists, who enjoyed very little political support in Flanders; the Walloonian municipality, however, granted them the right to march during the volatile aftermath of the shooting.

During the first season of *Jan Publiek*, the immigrant riot episode was the only one to draw such passion from the panelists that they at times cried out to be recognized by Van Rompaey, sometimes interrupting him or other panelists and guests. Sometimes, instead of waiting to be called on by Van Rompaey, panelists would directly reply to other panelists or guests who were addressing them. The videotape showed many instances of interactions that were much sharper than usual; occasionally Van Rompaey interceded to redirect to the specific issue at hand. In general, the polite, urbane character of *Jan Publiek* receded in favor of a robust but still mostly civil, if polarized, discussion.

Here is Betty, summing up the migrant riot situation concisely, in the censorious tone of her minilecture:

> What is awful is that all immigrants are treated the same way because of these incidents, but they are not all the same. There are five hundred hooligans but there are many others who are not like that. By reacting this way, you destroy

the good work of social workers and others who have tried to integrate the immigrants.

Betty was the only panelist whose speech provoked applause on this day, mainly from guests who represented the left and the immigrant community (the speech was stratified leftist), not from her fellow panelists, who were cast in the position of villains. Indeed, some of the panelists, led by the Vlaams Blok partisan Frans, expressed support for positions that were right-wing. Betty's rhetorical prowess meant that she knew the appropriate time to intervene in the discussion with one of her well-formed, paragraph-long lectures, and she did succeed in consolidating the opposition, so to speak. What she did not do was to open further discussion.

Rudi frequently interposed himself into the discussion. However, in this episode, Rudi did not employ the speech genres that showed him to be amiable as well as authoritative, and here his perspective sounded almost colonial—the opposite of Betty's. Simultaneously, he actually sounded more like Betty than ever, since one of his speech genres was a lecture. He also used more verdictives (that is, he made authoritative pronouncements). Yet it may be that Rudi's status as a gay man entered silently into the discussion. When Pym Fortuyn, an openly gay candidate for prime minister in Holland (next-door to Flanders), was making a name for himself, he had complained of being described by an imam as "worse than a dog" for being gay. (Fortuyn was later assassinated in 2002 by a crackpot on the political left.) Just what Rudi might have heard regarding Islam and homosexuality in 1997 we cannot know.

After a panelist expressed "horror" and "repulsion" at the video of the immigrant riots in Anderlecht, Rudi indicated to Van Rompaey that he wished to speak. As he spoke, he did not descend into the maelstrom of the melodrama ("horror," "repulsion"), but stood aristocratically above it. The stratification here is polite, middle-class Flemish and managerial.

> It is unacceptable behavior. They are our guests and they are not behaving like guests. They wouldn't be allowed to behave like this in their own country. I'm not a racist, but this is not acceptable.

Rudi also told a story from his position as employer. He said he had hired two Muslims ("through positive discrimination"), one of whom complained of racism whenever his bosses tried to discipline or instruct him. He continued:

> I say it respectfully that Arabs are still good merchants. They're very clever and I've experienced, as colleagues have told me too, that from time to time they use [the fact that they are immigrants to their advantage].

The well-formed nature of the authoritative speech (this is an expositive in which stereotypes are offered as evidence) and the calmness of the delivery were qualities that probably only served to incite his opponents. The stereotype was not offered melodramatically—indeed, "from time to time" is a qualifier, seldom employed in melodramatic discourse—but the use of "Arabs" is redolent with melodramatic potential.

A Muslim woman wearing traditional dress and a headscarf sat upright and spoke in brief utterances that partook of authoritative and moralistic speech genres on a par with those of Rudi and Betty. She also interrupted—after Van Rompaey had directly invited Fatiya to speak—to deliver a scornful rejoinder to Rudi's utterance: "When I hear something like this, I don't even think it's worth it to respond." Van Rompaey replied as though she meant this literally: "You don't have to, you don't have to." His mode seemed at once anxious and reassuring. This encouraged the Muslim woman to continue, and Rudi entered on his own, without the host's invitation:

Muslim woman: If you talk this cheap, I think if you talk this cheap—

Rudi (interrupting): That's the experience, miss.

Muslim woman: You have to look at—

Rudi (interrupting): It's all nice in pr—theory—but just try to do it in practice.

Muslim woman: Take a look at "I think people who are Arabs are good merchants."

Rudi: Ah, yeah.

Muslim woman: That's exactly the same as saying he's from Holland, he's stingy, and he's from Belgium, he's dumb.

Rudi: No, no.

Muslim woman: I mean, and there we are. That's not a discussion.

Rudi: But you're cunning.

Van Rompaey: Not everyone at a time. Betty?

Muslim woman (to Rudi): And you're not.

In this heated exchange, even though the speech genres themselves were broken up by the interruptions, the speakers managed to make their positions quite clear—too clear, too soon, perhaps, for a situation of confusion and upset. The Muslim woman was reproving Rudi, comparing his speech to that of other easy stereotypes traded between the Dutch and the Belgians. She pronounced from a superior position, and did bump Rudi off his high perch, although she did not persuade him. In fact, he made a meta-pronouncement about her rhetorical game ("But you're cunning"). Her response in kind confirmed the game.

Fatiya, however, made repeated attempts to be understood, and her utterances showed her to have herself attempted to understand others. Her speech genres told stories of her difficulties in becoming Belgian (she was born in Leuven and was a naturalized Belgian) and of the plight of others that she knew. She often represented the positions of others, be they immigrant or Belgian, with nuance and sensitivity. There was an exchange between Fatiya and Albert that suggests some of the possibilities of *Jan Publiek* in the way of encouraging serious dialogue on a controversial issue. A panelist, Albert, spoke excitedly (and in sentences that are not well formed), after waiting for Van Rompaey to call on him.

Albert: Yes, well, I've heard a lot of things. My neighbor Fatiya has said some interesting things on the one hand, but on the other hand she says that even her parents, the first generation, doesn't take a stand [against youth violence]. Now we blame our politicians and the police, and the immigrants as well, because it's our, well, everyone's . . . that they acted in a wrong way or that they didn't act at all. But where is the first generation then, because if they want things to change for their children, they have to be the first ones to reclaim political rights and they have to get on the streets, not demonstrating, but in a political way.

Van Rompaey: So what you mean is—

Albert: —in an intelligent way

Van Rompaey: —the first generation

Albert: —They're a lot older than those sixteen-, seventeen-year-olds we just heard [being interviewed on the pretaped sequence]—

Van Rompaey: Yes

Albert: But we don't see them, all we see is their children. I feel the immigrants are being defended by children.

Van Rompaey: Yes, Fatiya, is it—

Albert: —and the parents are hiding under the veil of Islam.

Van Rompaey: —Let's ask—

Albert: —and that's wrong. They have to take responsibility for their children, as I should do as well as others.

"[H]iding under the veil of Islam" strikes a melodramatic note that helps to position Muslim parents as villains (even as they are pretending to be victims), while Albert can be a hero. At this point, Fatiya could easily have taken umbrage and responded to Albert as the other Muslim woman did to Rudi, for Albert had cast aspersions on Fatiya's religion. But when she got her chance to speak, she used stories from her own experience to belie the assumptions of Albert and other panelists who had made similar criticisms. At first, her efforts enjoyed the support of Van Rompaey.

> Van Rompaey: Yes, Fatiya, that's true, you rarely see—
>
> Fatiya: Yes
>
> Van Rompaey: And I've even talked with older people in Anderlecht.
>
> Fatiya: Yes
>
> Van Rompaey: They don't want that, they want—
>
> Fatiya: Yes, well, first, if you'd meet my mother or father—I don't think my father speaks enough Dutch to say anything about that.
>
> Van Rompaey: It's about the responsibility of the children.
>
> Fatiya: Yes, they feel responsible as well, but on the other hand, they feel abandoned by the government.
>
> Van Rompaey: Yes
>
> Fatiya: Because when they try to take the law into their own hands, they [the government officials] say, "Oh, no, you can't raise children like that, because we do it like this. No, you can't do this or that"— or whatever, or "He has to go to a detention center." So the children sometimes abuse the first generation parents and that's why the first generation—because of language problem—and when their kids err—how shall I put this?—err, or is behaving like a hothead or whatever, then—

Fatiya and Van Rompaey seemed to be making headway in this new version of *Jan Publiek*, where a panelist could try to work through a problem, even occasionally in the interrogative ("how shall I put this?"), but then Albert butted in again, and Van Rompaey—perhaps sensing time elapsing—invited Fatiya back onto the floor, but only to set up a transition to a new segment.

> Van Rompaey: —becomes a criminal, or—
>
> Albert: —yes, becomes a criminal—so that's where the parent loses the power over—

Van Rompaey: Yes

Albert: But the parents absolutely disapprove of this, but—

Van Rompaey: Yes, and that's how a riot escalates, and we've seen those images since Saturday. [A prerecorded sequence begins to be shown on a screen
to the side of Van Rompaey's podium, depicting an imam singing amidst the
crowd of protestors.] Fatiya, I ask you, uh, what did the man sing?

Fatiya: Yes, he's an imam and I hear someone [on the *Jan Publiek* set] sighing
because people don't like to hear what he's singing—but it's an imam singing
a verse—

Van Rompaey: —nothing inciting, it's just, uh—

Fatiya: —It's not to incite. It's just a man who's touched by it [the situation]
and who wants—

Van Rompaey: —Yes, well. I've already said that we've seen quite a few images
of the riots and the question is how that affects people.

Fatiya had been required to reassure native Flemings that the imam was not
inciting violence, but she and Albert (and Van Rompaey) were derailed in
their attempts to understand why the first-generation immigrant parents have
a difficult time controlling their children. Fatiya's story implicitly criticized the
Belgian government and its policies regarding childrearing. The aesthetic and
politics of *Jan Publiek* did not seem to allow further investigation into what
seems a promising discussion. The show must go on, and, in this episode more
than many others, there was something of a script to follow.

Just at the point that Fatiya and Albert might have been able to compare
their perspectives, Van Rompaey interrupted to bring the conversation back
onto the track that he and his producers had laid before the program began
to broadcast. But here we have seen how Fatiya tried to dispel misapprehen-
sions with full and sympathetic attention to people's experience. She did not
attack Albert, who certainly could be made to pay for his ignorance of the
Muslim community. Earlier, she had spoken kindly of native Belgians, and
her interactions with them. She might have been able to fulfill the function
that Van Rompaey—and perhaps she herself—seems to have wanted, that
of a mediator (Van Rompaey obviously called on her, and not any of the
Muslim guests, to translate the imam's language). Here is one instance where
Nico Carpentier's criticism of *Jan Publiek* does seem warranted.

Participation is shown to be impossible without the management of a host (and
his production team) and highly constrained by the professional standards of

the broadcasters, whose main objective is to make a "good" programme, reducing participation to a secondary objective. (2001, 229–30)

Our perspective in this book is that hosts and production teams do fulfill an important function, and that there is nothing wrong with making a "good" program. Furthermore, we argue that a show always sets up an aesthetic that is also an ethic. Yet a talk show, with its elastic generic boundaries, might also be able to depart from its usual type on occasion. The "Migrant Riots" episode uncharacteristically delves into the melodramatic—not surprisingly, given the circumstances and the topic. Our citizen Jan or Jana Publiek might need or want to engage in that political aesthetic. But this kind of melodrama on a live audience discussion show does present some difficulties that *Jan Publiek*'s dominant political aesthetic seemed unable even to acknowledge, much less anticipate and address.

CHAPTER THREE

~

Showto Na Slavi of Bulgaria:
Vox Populi

Bulgaria offers a study on divisions between East and West. That there is not just one "East" and one "West" is clear in any cultural study of the country. First, there is the "East" of the Middle East and its difference from the "West" of Europe. Bulgaria was a part of the Ottoman Empire for about five centuries, ending in the late nineteenth century. Today one can still see the odd man in a full squat—an Eastern posture—while waiting for the bus, or one bearing a large load of cardboard for recycling high on his back, reminiscent of an Ottoman porter. Chalga music is the most popular music in Bulgaria at the moment, reviled by the educated for its quotations from the Turkish musical tradition, its trashiness, and its association with the current criminal elements in the country.

This brings us to the other main form of difference, within Europe, between Western and Eastern, capitalist democracies versus Communist totalitarianism. Bulgaria has had to negotiate both lines of difference, and everything symbolically that each division stands for, a large burden to bear for a historically small agrarian country. So many humiliations have been visited upon Bulgarians for so long that emotions are tangled and contradictory, and words, as Hamlet said, lose the name of action. The Bulgarians with the impetus to act are sometimes among the worst—mobsters, corrupt politicians, and their thuggish minions. Many ordinary Bulgarians believe that these "political" actors have stolen untold amounts of the people's money. Sometimes it seems as if they have stolen an entire nation, a nation that had already been either abandoned or exploited by the powers of both East and West.

Western capitalists are now rushing back in to "develop" this "backward" country, virtually destroying in a few years the beauty that was the Black Sea coast. The dismissive and paternalistic attitude of the new conquerors is everywhere apparent. It may be that the Bulgarians who care about "the West" have internalized these criticisms. But many Bulgarians seem to follow a practical (and historically Bulgarian) route of going underground, making fun of their overlords privately, focusing on their own survival and partaking of the available simple pleasures of life. And not a few Bulgarians, especially the young, are emigrating.

> Every year, there are 60,000 fewer Bulgarians due solely to the declining birth-to-mortality ratio. Mass unemployment, deteriorating health care, low incomes, the depopulation of rural areas, and inconsistent state policy are all to blame for the demographic crisis. If the present rates of decline persist, the Bulgarian nation is set to disappear by 2050–60, experts warn. (*World Press Review* 28)

One of the most important sources of hope these days is Bulgaria's entry into the European Union. This may help to curb the corruption, bring more EU funds into the country, and underwrite more responsible capitalist development, although this is hard to say. At the moment, Bulgarians are watching as entire villages are purchased by British nationals looking for a cheap place to retire.

The creators of *Showto Na Slavi* not only use the show to comment upon recent Bulgarian history, they have themselves taken part in that history. Slavi Trifonov and Luben Dilov Jr. have both been a part of comedy teams performing before the camera spanning the entire period of the fall of Communism—just before it, during, and now, after. Their first show *Cuckoo* satirized the Communist elite through the dialogue of two female prostitutes (played by two men in drag, one of whom was Trifonov). In 1995, *Canaletto* featured political satire, as did *Hushove*, named for Bulgarian nationalist leaders of the nineteenth century. Obviously, Trifonov and his colleagues saw themselves as presenters and interpreters of Bulgarian history and contemporary politics. They were at the ready during one of Bulgaria's darkest hours, the winter of 1996 when the economy bottomed out for the second time since the fall, with the Bulgarian leva plummeting in value hour by hour. People were going hungry. The man in power was Prime Minister Jean Videnov, one of a long string of politicians presiding over a corrupt government. Bulgarians have changed their government eleven times in eleven years in futile attempts to clean up the corruption (Dimitrov). The *Canaletto* team invented a chant, used by protesters during "Videnov's Winter." It involved the kind of clever wordplay for which Trifonov and company still remain famous.

Putniko viden [prominent traveller]
putniko off [travel off]

The chanters were telling Videnov "off"—the "off" in the rhyme stood for both the ending of Videnov's name and the English word "off"—and perhaps contributed to his removal from power.

Showto Na Slavi and Slavi Trifonov

Showto Na Slavi began in the year 2000, at almost the same moment as BTV, Bulgaria's first commercial television network, officially claimed one of the two previously state-run television studios. Not long after that, BTV was purchased by Balkan News Corp, a subsidiary of Rupert Murdoch's News Corp. This brought a much-needed infusion of capital into the station that benefited its phenomenally successful late-night television talk show *Showto Na Slavi*. In the early years of *Slavi*, including the year from which our episode is taken, 2003, one-third of all Bulgarians—not just those watching television—were tuned in to this late-night television talk show. It had created its own "second prime-time," according to MediaLinks, the independent company measuring television viewing in this new democracy. One of the cocreators of the program, impresario and sometime politician Lyuben Dilov Jr., son of a well-known science fiction writer, told our research team that *Slavi* was "a monster," one that achieved its extraordinary success because it had entered the scene at an auspicious historical moment. In 2003, Trifonov and the *Slavi* Cuckoo Band cut a CD that they titled *Vox Populi*. But even without that hint, it was clear from our interviews with then-coproducer Dilov Jr. and the show's scriptwriters that the creators of *Slavi* intended the show to represent the Bulgarian people—to remind them of their unique history and achievements, to depict Bulgarians speaking in the numerous Bulgarian dialects and from all walks of life, to enable them to speak back to the nation's politicians and elites and those of the world, to assist them in their present difficulties, and mostly, of course, to entertain them.

Making a Myth

In *Convergence Culture*, Henry Jenkins makes a large claim for fan fiction (stories written by fans in appreciation of commercial fiction such as *Star Wars*): "[F]ans envision a world where all of us can participate in the creation and circulation of central cultural myths" (256). This statement by Jenkins as well as others he has made throughout his distinguished career takes the

valuation of popular culture as far as it can possibly go from the utter denunciation it received from Adorno and Horkheimer in "The Culture Industry."
Yet it seems to us that it may be possible to overappreciate popular culture
merely because it is popular, or even because fans are moved by it in some
way. That would leave us scant room for making the kind of aesthetic and
ethical judgments this book attempts to make. In the case of myth, it certainly seems right to say that we all can participate in and circulate myths.
But to claim that just anyone can create a myth seems a stretch. Since the
word is Greek, perhaps *The Oxford Classical Dictionary* may be of help to us.
"No universally accepted definition of myth exists," writes contributor Jan N.
Bremmer, professor of history and religion at the University of Groningen,
Netherlands, "but Walter Burkert's statement that 'myth is a traditional tale
with secondary, partial reference to something of collective importance'
gives a good idea of the main characteristics of myth" (1018). Jenkins argues
for a "collective intelligence" at work in convergence culture, where thousands or even millions of fans participate interactively with media and with
one another (2). So, absent the history, perhaps popular culture could be a
place to begin a myth.

In the editor's introduction to Robert Graves's *The Greek Myths*, Kenneth
MacLeish reminds us (using the past tense) that myths offered

> not so much answers to particular questions as ways of beginning to think
> about answers—and the questions had to do with the nature of the universe,
> the relationship between human beings and the supernatural, the reasons for
> certain customs or ways of behavior and the self-image of this or that commu-
> nity. For adherents of particular cults or citizens of specific areas, myths offered
> a communal viewpoint, a focus for thought; they put people in touch not only
> with one another's minds but with those of their forebears and ancestors; they
> validated each present moment in terms of a much wider picture, both in time
> and space—they were a binding force. (11)

It seems to us, too, that the relation to history cannot be gainsaid. While
undoubtedly an impressive popular cultural phenomenon, *Star Wars*, in this
view, may be lacking on two counts, as it does not draw significantly upon
tradition, nor is its importance "collective," but rather—as Jenkins's concept
of fandom makes clear—it addresses a select niche of people. Finally, we
have Northrup Frye's statement: "In terms of narrative, myth is the imitation
of actions near or at the conceivable limits of desire" (136).

However, it does seem possible that new myths could arise and even that
they could do so from out of a commercial and pop context. We will argue
that the *Slavi Show* is far from being a mere copy of the *Tonight Show with*

Jay Leno—a claim made in this extreme form by a Bulgarian cultural studies scholar and made in milder form by the *Slavi* creators themselves. We believe that especially the character "Slavi," played by Trifonov both on- and offstage, strikes a mythic register. As such, his delineations and meanings are not always clear. We sometimes see in him a type of the trickster. The trickster is a morphing creature, "who is not guided by normal conceptions of good or evil, who is either playing tricks on people or having them played on him and who is highly sexed" (Radin 155). Radin points out that the trickster, wherever in the world he is found, is the subject and cause of "drastic entertainment." The trickster is an overreacher whose cunning is often a form of stupidity (Radin 180). The Native American coyote, for example, plucked out his eyes and tossed them over a tree in order to see further, only to lose his sight altogether. The trickster belongs to an archaic period, but many of his qualities appear in figures of more recent times. In the former Ottoman Empire, the Karagoz (Turkish) or Karagiosi (Greek) shadow theatre offered tricky heroes with large noses (to signify a large penis) who were perhaps derivatives of the trickster: "[T]he trickster has been a source of amusement right down to civilized times, where he can still be recognized in the carnival figures of Pulcinella and the clown" (Radin 204). Judging, however, by David Madden's descriptions of the characters of commedia dell'arte, Italian outdoor comedy popular from the sixteenth through nineteenth centuries, the trickster function might have been distributed across more than one character. Pulcinella (ancestor to the Punch of "Punch and Judy") is similar to Brighella, who is "dishonest, unscrupulous, opportunistic, malicious, vengeful, egotistic" (Madden 10). Pantaloon is a "miserly, overreaching, credulous, talkative, sententious old fool . . . the cuckholded husband of a passionate young wife and the deceived father of an eager virgin" (4). Harlequin—a dull-witted counterpart to Brighella and also ancestor to Punch—always carried a large stick (another phallic symbol). Madden's book compares commedia dell'arte with the silent film comedies of Chaplin, Keaton, Lloyd, and Oliver and Hardy. It is commedia dell'arte that furnished silent film with the epithet "slapstick"—the stick of Harlequin, often used to cudgel and penetrate people in various and creative ways.

For those accustomed to conceiving television purely in the terms of contemporary popular genre, "Slavi" is merely the wisecracking host of a late-night talk show. But if genre can be as broad as Bakhtin would have it, "Slavi" can also be a character of a type of comedy that has mythic dimensions; its borrowings take it well beyond what is currently known as "hybridity." Like all myth, this one is bent by and toward the particular local culture—a culture which some have dismissed as having nearly no culture at all (see Peckham 183).

Trifonov himself underwent changes in making himself into a modern-day myth. Formerly a tall, thin man, he bulked up, worked out, shaved his head, wore dark sunglasses, and presented himself generally as a *mutra* ("ugly face"), a bodyguard for the criminal "businessmen." Before Communism, the *mutra* had been Olympic athletes, seventy thousand strong in a country of only eight million. After 1989, they, like many other Bulgarians, were out of work and ripe for recruiting by the mafia. During the first decade of the post–Cold War period, it was the *mutra*, formerly ordinary men, who appeared to be "making it," driving expensive cars (usually SUVs), escorting beautiful young women to chalga parties, and using the first cell phones most Bulgarians had ever seen. Trifonov as "Slavi" became a spokesmen for MobilTel, the cell phone of the mafia. Trifonov's autobiography *Standing Tall* (playing on Trifonov's tall stature), or, in an alternate translation, *Standing Out Like a Sore Thumb*, featured Trifonov's face in extreme close-up, behind a broken glass spattered with blood. Whether Trifonov was confronting the mafia in his impersonation—the show often skewered them in its satiric skits, although, on the other hand, the show and the Cuckoo Band also welcomed chalga music—or suggesting that any means of survival should be boldly pursued by Bulgarians in extremis was unclear. From the point of view of satire, the current social scene was the main referent. It was on this level that the educated folk of Bulgaria judged the show. But from the point of view of myth, the referent was Bulgarians as a people, and humanity in general.

Both the appearance and the character of "Slavi" morphed continually. Sometimes he dressed like a legitimate businessman. On air, he played numerous Bulgarian characters, including a *hush*, a nineteenth-century revolutionary urging Bulgarian independence. "Slavi" was the fiancé of the prime minister's daughter (this was Prime Minister Simeon, who in infancy had been the tsar of Bulgaria). "Slavi" was also the husband of Temenushka, a frumpy and sexually aggressive village woman who deflated "Slavi's" machismo on a regular basis (see Dixon and Koleva, who argue that Temenushka is mythic and chthonic). Trifonov's own biography seems intended as much to contribute to the myth of "Slavi" as to provide public knowledge of Trifonov's background. The book takes the form of an interview between the two creators of "Slavi"—Dilov Jr. and Trifonov. In it, Trifonov's emergence from a village is played up. Although most Bulgarians are now urban dwellers, many still have important contacts in the village, and Bulgaria's agrarian history is central even to its contemporary identity. We talked with students in the capital city Sofia who looked down their noses at "Slavi"/Slavi's supposed village origins but also some who took pride in the thought. We take it as a deliberate attempt to plant "Slavi" in a Bulgaria that is at once historical and contemporary, a country with a history much deeper, more popular, and more complex than the Mother Bulgaria and the "folk" culture promulgated under Communism.

Whatever one might take "Slavi" to be, he clearly is energetic, dynamic, egoistic, and verbally precocious. Even though the show sometimes engages in vulgar humor—the humor ranges from high to low in almost every episode—and thereby offends those whose morality was formed under a dour Communism, most Bulgarians are fascinated by the show and by Trifonov, whose bald pate was (in 2003) seen everywhere on billboards, posters, and on the cover of a prestigious men's magazine as "Man of the Year."

Showto Na Slavi airs weeknights at the same hour as the *Tonight Show with Jay Leno* in the United States. *Slavi* exists in dialogue with the earlier shows by the same team (*Cuckoo, Canaletto, Hushove*), but when we talked to Dilov Jr., he confirmed that the show also was conceived in dialogue with the *Tonight Show with Jay Leno*. Certainly *Slavi* has the usual late-night talk show trappings: a wisecracking host, a sidekick, a band, and celebrity guests. But although Jay Leno's band's music is peppy, its energy and expressiveness is confined mainly to a brief buildup before and after the numerous commercial breaks, to mark the transition. Otherwise, the aesthetic of *Jay Leno* is tonally light, twinkling, relaxed; the polished political jokes of the monologue are mild, topical, and mainstream; the effect is to produce a genial sociality, an amusement, and perhaps a ritual preparation for bedtime. According to the taxonomers, late-night television talk shows are a different species from those thought formerly to contribute to democratic discourse, especially audience discussion shows. Talk on the late-night talk show is "chat."

By this typological reckoning, the *Slavi Show* confounds. It is a high-octane production of popular artists and political activists, not of stand-up comics or connoisseurs of chat (Rose). The monologue portion of the late-night talk show is modified by a reach back to television's predecessor, the stage. Like the variety show of the 1960s United States, *Slavi* borrows from the vaudeville-type entertainment, where the humor—sketches, skits, jokes, and gags—can be sharp or even "drastic." In the episode that we will analyze, 9 June 2003, there is a typical *Slavi* excess, not one introduction, but three—four, if one counts the performance of the dancers, who always help to open the show. Although the show is host-centered, as talk shows tend to be, on the *Slavi Show* the cast seems more of a troupe: host, band, dancers, and incidental sketch-actors tour the country together sometimes; the band cuts popular CDs (such as the previously mentioned *Vox Populi* from 2003). The monologue in which the sidekick Godji has a major role (and which sometimes involves cameo appearances by other comic actors) sprints right off the starting block into a thematically unified—albeit loosely so—integrated set of satirical sketches and jokes of political follies. No advertisements interrupt the flow of the program until the halfway mark, when they air in a block.

In the second half of the show, Slavi, who has been on his feet, sometimes propelling himself across the stage, sits calmly with a celebrity guest or someone drawn from the entertainment industry (musicians and actors are favored—Jean-Claude Van Damme, for example), or politicians (Mikhail Gorbachev, Wesley Clark), or, more rarely, ordinary people in extraordinary circumstances. Both Bulgarians and non-Bulgarians appear as guests (interpreters accompany those who do not speak Bulgarian). Although always graciously received, guests usually sit solo for a sometimes hard-hitting one-on-one interview, especially in the case of politicians. Always, international guests are required to address Bulgarian concerns; for example, Wesley Clark was pummeled with questions about the U.S. bombing of Serbia, a Christian Orthodox and Slavic country with which Bulgarians identify. The show's second half is also similar to many afternoon issue-oriented talk shows in its address to the personal. In the case of the *Slavi Show*, the personal is not only political but spiritual, borrowing from contemporary melodrama as well as older traditions while creating a new, mass-mediated set of rituals. In both halves of the show, the free, social (and masculine) spirit of the kritchma—the village tavern—is carried forward.

A studio audience sits on two sets of bleachers while the show is taped. They are not "warmed up" (Grindstaff) by any of the *Slavi* staff. On the evening of 9 June 2003, our research team sat in the studio audience. After having seen dozens of *Slavi* shows, we had all agreed that the formal nature of the program was important enough to deserve analysis. The text of *Slavi* seemed to us to be a whole. That is how we experienced it, as we sat expectantly in the BTV studio on a mild summer evening, prepared to engage in serious play.

Piling It On: A Bulgarian Popular Aesthetic

What Bulgarians see at home on their television sets and what we see onstage and on the monitors this evening is an introductory sequence drenched in contrasting, clashing colors accompanied by energetic movement and music. The blaring theme music is played while the title graphic *Showto Na Slavi* fills the television screen. The words appear on a three-dimensional gold medallion set within pulsating gold rings on a deep-blue background. The logo opens like a lid, and one of the five studio cameras moves closer to *Slavi*'s Cuckoo Band, seated before a solid backdrop of bright primary colors. On this night, the camera will frame the head and torso of "the Professor," the band's virtuoso clarinetist, who will greet the audience with a short speech, his upper body swaying musically, and introduce the comely young female dancers, attired in scanty and sporty outfits of hot pinks and blues. They begin their choreographed movements down a spiral staircase (located stage left) and cross the stage, as the camera follows them carefully from above for a few seconds before they are caught by another eye-level camera, which pans from left to right and back again, favoring center stage as a pausing point. The band plays an upbeat American pop song for the nine women to dance to, variety-show style, while lights from the ceiling play around them, and a Jumbotron screen behind and stage right oozes orange and red colors like an enormous 1970s lava lamp. The camera angle and range varies; no shot is held longer than two seconds. The dancing is athletic, sexually suggestive, and at times reminiscent of the playground (a pyramid is briefly formed), but the dancers' bodies are mainly contributing to abstract formations, viewed from mid- to fairly long shots. A controlled energy and formal beauty—contradicted by the garish colors—carries through the dance sequence.

The camera cuts to another upper-torso shot of Godji, Slavi's sidekick and a guitarist in the band, who offers a second introduction. It is prolonged and marked by an emphatic speaking style that almost hurls the language forth. Godji's face, too, is animated as he introduces the theme of the evening, holding aloft a newspaper clipping of Prime Minister Simeon's plans to build a tunnel in the Balkan Mountains. "Bravo!" he exclaims and plants a kiss on the clipping. Even more emphatically, he introduces the host: "Sla-vi Tri-fonov!" Now Slavi descends the staircase with a pick-axe over his shoulder, dressed as a brigadier.

What we have here is an aesthetic of hyperbole, of eclecticism, accumulation, and making do. The average Bulgarian home is cluttered with the odds and ends of things that used to work or be in style but that now await recycle. Lighting in public buildings is often dim to save electricity. Meanwhile, the out of doors of this formerly Communist country is gray from too much concrete architecture, dirt, and just plain lack of paint. The *Slavi Show* comes to the rescue as a kind of Bulgarian urban renewal project, bringing together even clashing colors, as though everything had to be used, every resource had to be put into play to oppose the enforced spiritual stagnancy of the past and the dreariness of the impoverished present. As we have said, the characters that Slavi inhabits are often hyperbolic too (e.g., the mafia boss, the beefcake ladies' man). But while the show, its website, and "Slavi" in his many avatars sometimes extol the virtues of capitalism (in opposition to Communism, perhaps), the show is also suffused with irony. The roles

"Slavi" plays often show him to be the "stupid" trickster: he drops his mous-tache and (figuratively) his pants on many occasions. The show's aesthetic belies the necessity of Western capitalism as the seat of the good life at least as much as the discourse supports it. The *Slavi Show* attempts to reinvigorate Bulgaria by representing, and often satirizing, the present, while attempting almost visceral ties with a Bulgarian but also a human past that the present often effaces or denigrates.

Opening Ritual: Greetings and Introductions

Each of the show's greetings—including the floating of the title medallion, the theme music, and the dance—has the illocutionary effect of opening the show. Because they involve "characters" and speech genres that the audi-ence knows and anticipates to a large extent, and because (we will argue) the show has important symbolic meaning for Bulgarians, the speech genres of the opening take on the nature of a ritual. What Fiske says about ritual on television will help us here.

> Levi-Strauss distinguishes between games and rituals by defining games as cul-tural forms in which participants start out equal and finish differentiated into winners and losers, whereas rituals take differentiated groups and provide them with equalizing communal meanings or identities. (165)

Perhaps because there is simply little Bulgarian-produced evening televi-sion programming, the *Slavi Show* draws its audience in part by invoking viewers as Bulgarian. The title is flashed in glitzy fashion in Bulgarian; most evening fare will have subtitles and will require some effort at cultural trans-lation. In dialogue with other television fare, the *Slavi Show* takes the almost internally differentiated Bulgarians, who are required to attend to so many global others, and provides them with a communal identity. Here, Bulgarians are home, as it were. And it is a nice home, finally; one they can be proud of when the guests arrive, as they literally do in the show's second half, in the form of international celebrities and politicians. All of the associations with the *Slavi Show* are associations of success: this is not the cheap production of most Bulgarian television fare, including some of the Western European im-ports. "Slavi" is by now almost a brand name, associated again with the New Bulgaria of freedom and opportunity—the good side of the "fall"—but full of irony and Bulgarian black humor so that it is still recognizable to mature Bulgarians. The audience is directly addressed as "dear viewers" twice before Slavi ever emerges. This suggests an intimacy, appropriate for the televisual medium and for talk shows in general (televisions are found in people's living rooms, and talk show sets usually mimic the living room), but also a ritual formality that we will see again at the show's close.

Speech Genres Recycled and Reaccented: The Communist Testimonial

When Godji takes over for the Professor, he assists in performing the ritual opening of the show. As usual, the audience is first addressed intimately as "dear viewers." Then, they'll be poised for a surprise and a need to work out a problem: Which ephemeral character is Godji playing tonight? What is his function for the show? The audience knows Godji's basic character—he is both a support and an obstacle to Slavi's own trickster character. Most likely Godji will introduce a theme for this episode, probably stemming from current events in Bulgarian politics. The illocutionary effect of this opening is like the drawing back of the curtain: the substantive portion of the show has begun. Get ready for the delight of political satire!

The home audience sees Godji in the same frontal mid-shot that framed the Professor's introductory speech. This time, we can see an elegantly dressed female singer behind and above Godji's right shoulder and a more drably dressed male saxophonist behind and to the left. Godji himself has the look of a hip artist in a brown silk shirt, small silver hoop earrings, a shaven head, and stubble on his face. His delivers his speech in an energetic and expressive manner, but not as histrionically as Slavi will do. The illocutionary effect of this part of the performance, then, is to make Godji the leader of an ensemble. Soon he will introduce his fellow performers. During Godji's opening monologue, a second or third camera cuts away to various band members to catch their reactions to the humor and artistry of his performance.

Although they will need to wait until the middle of Godji's monologue to discover the theme of tonight's show, most adult Bulgarians (indeed, most adult Eastern Europeans) will be able to discern relatively quickly the speech genre that Godji parodies. We will analyze it below.

> Good evening, dear viewers. My modest life experience has taught me that in order to develop as a balanced personality I have to combine mental and physical labor. Every night for the show's sake I mercilessly explore my gray cells and I strain my cerebellum until it starts sizzling like a Serbian barbecue. To tell you the truth, I am tired of intellectual labor. I said to myself, enough, let the muscle cell dominate the brain: I need the balance which only that primitive hard physical labor can give me. I feel like digging the foundations,

pouring cement, slaking lime: I feel like having tan lines, I feel like working my ass off. I have been waiting so long to replace the bass guitar with a strong chromium-plated hoe and now I have the opportunity. The brigadier movement is reviving! Here, take a look: "Simeon will support building a tunnel under the Balkan Mountains." Bravo, Mr. Prime Minister! We thank you for this initiative. I can guarantee that the whole Cuckoo Band will rise like a tidal wave to flow over the construction sites of the Motherland.

According to Bakhtin, a parody would be reaccentuation of an earlier utterance—in this case, the Communist testimonial. All but the youngest of Bulgarians will have experienced it firsthand, under compulsion. The state required such language on many occasions, including the times when it conscripted party members for the "voluntary" labor brigades, i.e., the Brigadier Movement. Bulgarians were called on to build the infrastructure that made possible the industrialization and modernization of the country, arguably Communism's greatest achievement, one that is not without its spiritual costs.

We have all seen the heroic posters of Communist realism, glorifying well-muscled workers with shirt-sleeves rolled. This "worker" Godji does not just work (or indeed, pose for a socialist portrait); he speaks. And how. His ethos begins in a confession of humility, as required by the bosses, apparently ("my modest life experience has taught me"), but thereafter, the speech itself ironically swells and soars. Our satirical wag is a master of isocolon ("I feel like digging the foundations, pouring cement, slaking lime"), crazy simile (his brain "sizzling like a Serbian barbecue"), and hyperbole ("rising like a tidal wave"). He swaggers in his range of diction (from "cerebellum" to "ass"), and he knows how to raise a climactic conclusion ("I can guarantee that the whole Cuckoo Band will rise like a tidal wave to flow over the construction sites of the Motherland"). Tucked into all this is a bit of sarcasm ("Bravo, Mr. Prime Minister, bravo!")—just in case the dullard elites have not figured out what to do with all this verbal virtuosity.

The perlocutionary effect on the audience is to bind them into an identity with this performer, this performance. Rhetorically speaking, it operates through both an expressive and persuasive mode. Not only does the audience experience the cathartic purge of negative emotions associated with dramatic and comedic performances, they also get to participate in a new political embodiment through their cocreation of this parody (as in Fiske's "semiotic democracy," 95) and through their approving laughter. They join with the Cuckoo Band as new Bulgarians, a people who are not "stupid peasants," but clever, knowing, and capable of confronting past indignities with zestful pleasure. Indeed, they must be internally persuaded (to use Bakhtin's term) to believe this, for Communist leaders elevated urban work at the considerable expense of centuries-old peasant culture, on which lay Bulgaria's main source of livelihood and identity. Even today, Bulgarians often call one another "stupid" and proclaim "I am not a peasant!" The character that performs the parody of the Communist testimonial is well beyond suspicion and defensiveness; he is, indeed, in command—and yet he remains an ensemble player. The ensemble is an important thematic (developing the brigadier movement), dialogic (the exchange between Godji and the band members; Godji and the audience; Godji and Bulgarian history, both recent and removed), illocutionary act (his speech and performance enacts the ensemble), and perlocutionary act (his speech and performance causes the audience to participate in his creation of the ensemble).

Godji establishes the ensemble through storytelling, weaving a tale of the brigadier movement that stars all the members of the Cuckoo Band. "I can well imagine how Dessi, Alex, and Lily Yoncheva"—the camera cuts to mid-shot frames of them smiling in response—"throw away their lacy costumes and get into quilted jackets. You watch them: beauty queens, but cranes, they preen," he jokes in poetic diction. "I can as well imagine this refined virtuoso, the Maestro"—the camera cuts to the bandleader, who sways as though strutting—"an Arda fag tucked into the corner of his mouth, a newspaper hat on his head, swearing at a bag of Zlatna Panega cement." Godji and the camera include the whole band in the satiric transformation of musicians into construction workers. It has connections with the outside world, symbolized by Godji's reference to an American jazz-pop musician ("The Professor . . . cr[ies] out from time to time: 'Snap to it, Iota, what are you gaping at, like Kenny G at the quicklime?'"). And it has an oversized, sometimes ridiculous "leader": "This whole work team, though, cannot be left without a brigadier-leader, and that's why I'll call him. Ladies and gentleman, the construction worker from Uchin Dol, the earth-shattering trowel from Pleven, the seventh-rank showman, Slav-ii Trifo-nooooov!"

One of the reasons that a good performance is so important to the ends of rhetoric—that is, to political persuasion and invitation to action—is not only that the audience is involved in a "nowness," but that their attention is focused, riveted in a way that, in ordinary consciousness, it rarely is. Any good performer will tell you that timing is everything. The performers of *Showto Na Slavi* make use of the same performance excellence that one sees on the *Tonight Show With Jay Leno* or any other show with what we might call classic entertainment standards. As the Cuckoo Band and the camera crew prepare for the appearance of Slavi, their actions crescendo and coordinate perfectly to build the excitement that will center on the "star." Although the show is not particularly high in what are known as production values, the camera crew knows how to move in on Godji to create an intensification of his image while he utters these final words of introduction. Simultaneously, he slows down his speech and raises his voice. The Cuckoo Band becomes one unit from their dispersed and casual position as audience manqué. They attack the first note of the *Slavi* theme song, crescendoing as they play a falling five-note series that rises in one-note steps to a loud, trumpet-shrilling conclusion. As the music steps both down and up, so does Slavi Trifonov, down the staircase but "up" to center stage. This is one tight ensemble.

The audience can expect Slavi to make a grand entrance, sufficient to his mythic ego and trickster nature. He does, beginning at the top of the staircase with the pulsating lights, stage left. The dancers have pivoted forward to stand at attention with saluting arms. And the surprise: Slavi appears in his usual host's evening suit, but this time with a beret, moustache, and pick-axe—a brigadier. He acknowledges the dancers as part of the ensemble by kissing the hand of one of them, acknowledging also her sexual desirability, and refurbishing one of his many "Slavi" trickster incorporations—ladies' man. He strides truculently to center stage and lunges toward the studio audience in rough greeting, swinging his pick-axe. As he turns to greet his sidekick Godji and barks another combative greeting, his moustache pops off. The audience laughs.

Rhyming Reportage and Repartee

In addition to the energy of Slavi's performance that we hope we have already captured, we would like to foreground the sense of spontaneity and dialogue that this scripted program offers. Slavi Trifonov's background is in improvisational acting and comedy; the audience knows that he is capable of surprises. The springy moustache that provokes laughter and insight—the audience can literally see through Slavi's performance in Brechtian, and perhaps carnival, fashion—provides a spontaneity that continues in the greeting to the home and studio audience.

> Thank you. Good evening, ladies and gentleman of the Labor BTV. Good evening to you, builders of New Bulgaria in our brigadier studio. Good evening to you from Isperih. I am glad to see you. Welcome students from Hristo Botev High School, Isperih. [He reads aloud the slogan on the placard raised by the students: "We want in Slavi's Show/Isperih to have a go!" In Bulgarian: Iskame v shouto na Slavi Isperih da se proslavi. Literally: We want to be famous on the *Slavi Show*.] Bravo, that's the way to do it, bravo! I'm glad to see you. . . .

Slavi greets the entire audience, home and studio, as "builders of New Bulgaria." He invites the audience to play along with the comedy troupe in its political satire. Although the phrase "builders of the New Bulgaria" is intended ironically (the ridicule of Prime Minister Simeon has already commenced), it is also sincere; as the audience joins with the troupe, they in fact embody a New Bulgaria, one that, at least in imagination, creatively and energetically embraces its newfound democracy.

And as this is Trifonov's first meeting with the studio audience—the rehearsal of this evening's program has been closed—there is a certain suspense. Whom in the audience will he notice? And a certain pleasure in the choice: a group of ebullient youngsters who offer themselves as a unified group. According to ratings experts, the youth are the strongest supporters of the *Slavi Show*; symbolically, they represent the future of the country. To the extent that viewers identify with them, the Hristo Botev High School students represent the whole of the audience, the future of Bulgaria. In this action as in many others, the *Slavi Show* has effectively chosen to engage in a dialogue with their audience of ordinary Bulgarians.

The Hristo Botev High School students have captured Trifonov's attention by creating a rhyming slogan that sounds a little like something from the *Slavi Show* scriptwriters' bag of tricks. Indeed, later in this evening's episode Slavi and Godji will satirize the government's coddling of a Russian-born underworld figure, Michael Chorni.

> Chorni brought back in discrete
> The court keeps mum like a hypocrite
> Some people got some money concrete
> Other people got screwed indeed
> And the situation came up real neat.
>
> [Chorni vurnat diskretno,
> Sudut mulchi koketno,
> Edni hora vzeha pari konkretno,
> A na drugi hora im vleze direktno,
> I polozhenieto stana perfektno.]

The doggerel exists as a dialogue between poetic and journalistic language—a mixture of "high" and "low" cultures—and achieves some of its humor through the disjunction. Although the students do not attempt political satire, it is clear that they mean to engage in a dialogue with the show in terms of its repeated speech genres. They mean to take part in the fun and parody of the carnival atmosphere. Slavi could hardly help but notice the students: they carry on the larger "theme" of the show. One more thing: the last line of the Chorni poem is an improvisation of Trifonov's, and adds to the sense of spontaneity or nowness of the moment. The entire dialogic of the performance demonstrates how the *Slavi Show* both encourages a "nowness," a present-tense interaction between the show and its viewers, as well as a democratic discourse that enables a specifically Bulgarian identity and a joyous self-expression and even self-promotion—which is also an internal dialogic of Slavi's character.

More Repartee and Ensemble

As is perhaps typical of the host-sidekick relationship on late-night talk shows, we see Godji both supporting Slavi's central role and undercutting it. In the opening sallies, Slavi's high energy and "bossiness" are apparent in his demands upon, and interruptions of, Godji. Meanwhile, Godji manages to insert jocular asides:

> Slavi: Please show again this piece of information. I want to see it to get inspired for heroic deeds. Read this signal sentence to me.
>
> Godji: [Reads from a newspaper clipping] "The Prime Minister will support building a tunnel under the Balkan Mountains."
>
> Slavi: Who?
>
> Godji: Simeon.
>
> Slavi: What's he going to do? [speaking over Godji]
>
> Godji: Your father-in-law. [Slavi's continuing "character" on the show is supposed to be engaged to Simeon's beautiful daughter.] Will support building a tunnel under the Balkan Mountains.
>
> Slavi: Bravo, bravo, Mr. Prime Minister. You might have lost your Spanish passport but you haven't lost your Bulgarian brigadier spirit. That's how it goes: in the past we had Hainboaz, now we'll have Simeonboaz. And from today NMSII will stand not for the National Movement Simeon II but for the National Movement Construction Armed Forces.

Godji does not just act as Slavi's straight man; he is both an enabler of Slavi's braggart ways and a diminisher. Slavi suggests that Simeon is ineffectual (it is hard to believe this tunnel will be built), corrupt (if the tunnel is built, it will be on the people's backs, as were such projects under Communism), and a poser (he had a Spanish passport—is he even Bulgarian?) who will carry on a history of exploitation from without ("we had Hainboaz"—a Turkish word—"now we'll have Simeonboaz"). But Godji suggests that Slavi himself may be corrupt (Simeon is his father-in-law) as well as a fantastic braggart, for everyone knows that Simeon's daughter has another fiancé.

> Godji: Bravo, well done, boss.
>
> Slavi: Call me "brigadier" from now on.

Godji: Well, yeah, but you look like a field keeper at a class reunion.

Slavi: But I am a brigadier, at least I think I look like one. And from personal experience I know that when the Tsar promises something he does it instantaneously. That's why I am pretty sure that right now the yellow brigades of the NMSII are already at the construction site and are building the architectural future of the country. Moreover, I know, Evgeni Dimitrov, Brigadier, Maestro, are you ready?

Evgeni: Yes.

Slavi: Yell at the mike, don't just sit there with those hairy arms of yours. Well, then, Evgeni likes, he says, having a tanline. I have seen him. What a body, what a colossus, like the Colossus of Rhodes [at these words, the camera is on Evgeni, who stands and poses monumentally]. Right. I know already what the first day was like. First workday, pervii rabochii den. [Evgeni plays a Russian song.] What was that, Evgeni? Ah, it is "Play, Concertina, Play." [Evgeni begins the song at the electronic keyboard set to sound like an accordion.] That's right, go on playing dear brigadier, young man, Evgeni. In this way, their foreheads sweaty, Yuliana Doncheva and Nina Chilova—[contemporary Bulgarian fashion-plate celebrities]—are pushing spades into the hard soil and keep saying: "The NMSII woman are no longer jades, they're spades." Ha ha ha.

"First workday" is a phrase from the Communist period intended to transform Bulgarians into socialist workers. The frequently played Russian song "Play, Concertina, Play" was probably intended to be inspirational, like a Woody Guthrie folk song, but probably felt more like a foreign chain-gang song to the conscripted Bulgarians.

All the while that Slavi is speaking about first workday, band members are singing along with Evgeni, as though they are all happy workers at the brigadier site. They form an ironic ensemble as they do so (that is the illocutionary effect) and we suppose that the perlocutionary effect is to invite the audience into the ironic work brigade. As they recognize the joke, they will almost surely be singing along—in some sense—themselves. This binds them socially to the *Slavi* cast, and also puts them onstage, so to speak, as public performers of political satire. In this way, the *Slavi Show* both speaks *for* the audience—who may not yet feel able to speak out publicly on their own—and *with* them.

The Traveler's Tale

A large mahogany desk sits before a wall with a window offering a "view" of the night sky, stars twinkling. This is a standard set for the interview portion of late-night talk. There is, however, a cupboard, whose bright yellow and green shelves—colors still garish and clashing—display a number of objects. Slavi's upper torso is visible above the desk and is often framed exactly in between the cupboard and the window. The performance in the second half of the show slows considerably. Slavi generally stays seated and matches his mood to what is usually a more serious, nonsatirical interview. On this occasion, the young guest may prompt the audience to revisit its economic difficulties and diasporic family relations.

The one guest for the evening is a Bulgarian Formula One race car driver who moved to Italy to pursue his sport. Georgi is fifteen with short but fashionably spiked hair (Slavi makes a joke comparing him to the Bulgarian equivalent of a Chia pet, whose moistened clay head grows grass). He has poise but speaks about his young and eventful life in a quiet voice, almost in monotone. The illocutionary effect is to create a "real," honest, sincere report from the front, so to speak. Indeed, the quiet and the relevance of the topic—the local dialogic operating here is that almost all Bulgarians have family or friends who have emigrated—draws the audience in, as though straining to hear a whisper. Even Slavi seems to lose his actor aura (Trifonov has often claimed to feel least comfortable during the interview portion of the show). Although Georgi says he speaks Italian in daily life, on this night he speaks Bulgarian with Slavi, so there is no translator.

One way to analyze the speech genre is to think in terms of the interview, clearly in dialogue with other late-night talk shows—indeed, with almost all other talk shows. But if myth was visible in the first half through the character of "Slavi," it is present in the second half through folktale and ritual. The interview is merely the vehicle for conveying these. Propp's folktale portrays the ordinary person in his or her extraordinary or cosmic dimensions. In addition to the riotous performances at carnival, there have long been quieter ones at the hearth. In these scenes, a storyteller, known personally to the auditors and more or less talented, usually engaged the audience in light diversions, homely moral instruction, or, on the highest plane, the art of myth: stories to explain the world and to offer guidance in one's life. In the United States, some afternoon talk shows like the *Oprah Winfrey Show* draw on this ancient tradition, but it is rare that a late-night talk show will do so. As on *Oprah*, Slavi's interview with Georgi can merge myth with melodrama and its sometimes sentimental "happy ending" (Neale and Krutnik). However, in this episode, the camera generally retains a respectful distance whether framing Georgi or Slavi or the two together.

The story that is woven is a version of Propp's folktale: a boy must leave his family to solve a problem—here, lack of money and opportunity. He encounters trials and obstacles but eventually returns triumphant. The myth is in keen dialogue with the lives of contemporary Bulgarians, many of whom must emigrate for well-paying jobs, usually sending money home to their strapped families. Georgi has returned. He and Slavi take a look at his Formula One racing car, which has been rolled onto the stage, treasure from abroad, and the "magical agent." Slavi's questions emphasize the return. The studio audience is rapt.

> Slavi: Do you often come to Bulgaria? For how long? Now you've come to be my guest, otherwise do you often come back to Bulgaria? You have lived in Italy for the last three years, so—
>
> Georgi: I have lived in Italy for the last three years but I miss Bulgaria a lot. . . .
>
> Slavi: Do you think in Italian now or in Bulgarian?
>
> Georgi: Yes, I think in Italian but still there is part of me at home that thinks in Bulgarian.

Slavi continues to ask the kinds of questions that will flesh out this story. The obstacles and knowledge gained: "How did you get in touch with it [the Italian karting concern]?" "How did they let you participate?" "How did you enroll in such a school?" Part of the perlocutionary effect is to inform Bulgarians about the world, as in self-help or civic affairs discourse, but by far the main effect is to cause the audience to place his or her life struggle within the realm of myth. The audience may also be more literally invoked as vicarious or potential world travelers, or—as this comment suggests—as "supporters" of those going abroad to make good: "So all your family supported you and went to Italy with you so that you can have such a career?"

In the tale of old, the hero always returns home for good, marries the princess, and restores the lost order to the community. But Georgi will not move back to Bulgaria. His actions during the closing ritual are therefore all the more poignant.

Closing Ritual: Proverbs and Benedictions

It is at the conclusion of the interview that we see the ritual significance of the cupboard before which the camera carefully frames Slavi during a good part of the second half of the show. The speech genres, too, participate in a ritual interaction. Slavi and Georgi take their leave of one another as though in preparation for a serious undertaking. If the set had become the hearth during most of the interview, it has now become a dais upon which solemn, public exchanges can be made. Slavi now takes on the role of elder, bestowing blessings and directing the ceremony. Georgi soon joins Slavi as an able leader and bearer of symbolic tokens. The audience clearly is intended as recipient.

Slavi: I wish you luck. I most sincerely believe that you'll make it.

Georgi: Merci.

Slavi: I'm positive about that.

Georgi: Vanka, [referring to one of the show's personnel] you can bring it. I have a present for you.

Slavi: OK. Vanka will come but I will tell you what Niki Lauda said. He claims that the most important rule of driving is not to be a part of the car but to be one with it. As I am listening to you, I am convinced that you are one with your car and you'll have further success. I wish you luck from the bottom of my heart. Vanka, come here, please.

Georgi: So I have this. This is the first cup that I won in Italy. It's connected with lots of emotions and I would like to leave it with you because I think that it should stay in Bulgaria, that cup. And I have also brought you this pair of torn gloves that have seen lots of races.

Slavi: Thank you, my friend. As I respect you, I'll put this cup right here [on shelves behind his seat which are reserved for gifts from guests], and it will stay right here with me. I will ask you to put down something in our book.

Georgi: Of course.

Slavi: Here you are [passes him the guestbook]. [The Cuckoo Band plays contemporary inspirational music while Georgi signs the book.]

Slavi: Would you read it for us?

Georgi: It's a piece of advice that I would like to give to lots of people. And it's true for me and one should be very careful. So I wrote: "Never drive faster than your guardian angel can fly."

Slavi: Ladies and gentleman, tonight a young Bulgarian was my guest, whom we all wish luck. Thank you, Georgi, bless your soul, thank you very much.

Georgi does as many other guests have done, judging from the objects on the shelves behind Slavi: he offers a gift, one that has especially high symbolic significance, a trophy for his first major achievement, an achievement made as a Bulgarian youth. This is an excercitive, in Austin's parlance, "the exercising of powers, rights, or influence" (151); in this case, Georgi bequeaths the trophy. Slavi responds with a commissive, a promise ("it will stay right there with me") (151). This ritual exchange is capped by another, the offering of an adage that is meant as real advice (what Harnish means when he says proverbs are "directive," 269) and as a blessing (an Austin behabitive, a "reaction to other people's behavior and fortune"). Another behabitive ends this segment, as Slavi speaks for all of the Slavi community, wishing another Bulgarian good luck. All along one assumes the audience has been invoked, but quite explicitly when Georgi offers his advice ("It's a piece of advice that I would like to give to lots of people") and when Slavi directly addresses the audience and speaks on their behalf: "Ladies and gentleman, tonight a young Bulgarian was my guest, whom we all wish luck." There is something of a benediction in Slavi's final pronouncement ("bless your soul"). After this quiet moment comes an advertisement, one more joke, and one last direct address to the audience, inviting them to visit the *Slavi Show* online. Finally, Slavi puts his hands together in prayer, bends at the waist in a bow, and says, "It was an honor to have you as my guests."

Our analysis has leaned heavily upon the performative, which is the means by which the ritual engages the audience. But we hope we have made it clear that Bakhtin's contextual dialogic is still in full operation. This particular ritual makes its appearance and carries its force only in this particular time and place. In fact, we can report that three years later, in 2006, the *Slavi Show* had omitted the guestbook ritual altogether.

Proverbial Pleasure and Wisdom

Although not technologically deficient in comparison to most late-night talk shows, the *Slavi Show* puts the emphasis on performance (music, dance, acting), on verbal wit and dexterity, and upon audience-invoking ritual. Some of the speech genres also exist in dialogue with older genres and traditions, as in the case of the doggerel in rhyming couplets—taken from both journalism and older poetic forms—that the Isperih High School students imitate. At the show's ending, another traditional speech genre is given pride of place: the proverb, or wise saying.

The *Slavi Show* has often drawn from the National Revival period in Bulgarian history (late nineteenth century), a time that most Bulgarians celebrate as their liberation from Ottoman rule. Trifonov often plays a character from this time—a *hush*, a hero that instigates the rebellion. It is an ironic portrayal, for the rebellions were ruinous failures; Bulgaria's "freedom" came through Russian influence—with strings attached, of course. As the name suggests, this period also saw a conscious revival of Bulgarian culture. It was a time of the blossoming of written literature, history, and art (see Vazov for a fictional portrayal—and a literary exemplification—of this period). The *Slavi Show* means to do this, to revive a Bulgarian past and to remake a Bulgarian identity for the present. Its deliberate embeddedness in history provides an emotional depth that many first-world "issue-oriented" talk shows cannot offer, a sense of rootedness and continuity in the midst of upheaval and dissolution.

Georgi's proverb has resonances with a whole trove of Bulgarian sayings and blessings (Vazov's novel illustrates this well). These have endured even when written Bulgarian all but disappeared during Ottoman times, and when Soviet-style repression determined the content of public expression. To be sure, proverbs are generally passed down from elder to youth, and this one travels the other direction—the youth giving advice to the elders is a sure sign of modernity. Nonetheless, the ritual still carries: Bulgarian hosts and guests must discharge their responsibilities to one another—must, thereby, seal the social pact that has been entered into. Georgi must give gifts. They are, symbolically, gifts of promise (the trophy) and wisdom (the proverb). Slavi too speaks carefully and formally, and offers a benediction both to Georgi, whose story, after all, has only just begun, and to the audience, whose stories continue, with endings still deferred.

The *Slavi Show* and Talk Show Scholarship

As we have seen, Carpentier laments that the "main objective" of the Belgian audience discussion program, *Jan Publiek*, "is to make a 'good' programme, reducing participation [of the ordinary Flemings who constitute the panelists] to a secondary objective" (229–30). But I doubt the audience, also comprised of ordinary Flemings, and who made the show very popular, shared his perspective. Similarly, the studies in Tolson's recent *Television Talk Shows* reduce the meaning of rhetoric and artistry to "management of 'lay' and 'expert' discourses" (Wood 65) and "different forms of entertainment" (Brunvatne and Tolson 154) and "entertainment through talk" (Haarman 31). But this focus on entertainment merely serves to continue the old divide between high and low culture, and to preserve the cultural studies bias against aesthetics. The *Slavi Show* soundly rebukes such perspectives, since its entertainment is also art, an art that is both mythic and political.

The *Slavi Show* demonstrates not only that talk show talk is not simple (as Tolson and many other talk show scholars have shown), but that artistry and political rhetoric are of a piece. It engages its home and studio audience in Bakhtinian dialogue on contemporary global and local affairs, and does so in further dialogue with Bulgarians' shared past (troubled though rooted) and in view of their uncertain future. Bulgarian guests and audience participate through, not in spite of, the show's artistry. They stand to be entertained, surely, but also to be enriched and enabled in the process. Through the *Slavi Show*, they find a means of imagining a vibrant public sphere that exists on a larger world stage, one that significantly includes the usually overlooked or denigrated Bulgarian.

Slavi at his interview spot, trophy case to his right (courtesy of the Bulphoto Agency).

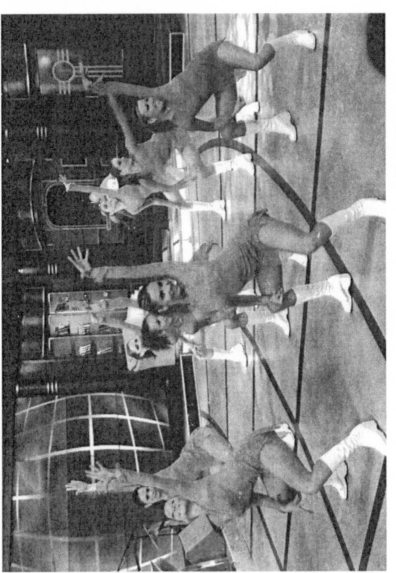

The Megadance troupe that opens and closes every show (courtesy of the Bulphoto Agency).

~

CHAPTER FOUR

The *Oprah Winfrey Show* of the United States: Melodramatic Citizen

This chapter analyzes particular episodes of a U.S. afternoon television talk show—the *Oprah Winfrey Show*—that were able to do what network evening news programs found difficult: focus the attention of a sizeable audience on matters of serious civic concern for an hour at a time. Winfrey and her creative team are to be credited with this achievement. They understand one of the most important components of rhetoric: know your audience. As well, they understand how rhetoric is to be conducted on the televisual medium. Once denigrated for its feminine and/or "trashy" nature, Winfrey and her creative team found that the afternoon talk show was an unusually flexible genre. Their continual transformations over the years have virtually defined the genre. Finally, in sizing up their audience and the demands of the medium, they also know how to use the "heterogeneous" aesthetic (Gledhill) of melodrama that taps into the deepest needs of the audience.

Our interest in the *Oprah Winfrey Show* is primarily with the civic-oriented episodes that were broadcast in the middle of George W. Bush's second term as president of the United States. It was at this point that the popular and long-running show began to move away from a studiously nonpartisan political perspective toward one that was overtly liberal. Where before politicians from both mainstream political parties appeared on the show—usually questioned on personal topics, as though they were A-list celebrities—during 2006 Barack Obama not only appeared on the show but was endorsed by Winfrey in his presidential bid. This was an unusual move by Winfrey—and it cost her some of her legendary popularity (Keeter)—but the other civic-oriented episodes that aired that season were unusual as well. They may have been a response in part to the Bush administration's take-no-prisoners rhetoric leading up to the second Iraq war, and the administration's alliance with Murdoch's right-wing Fox News Network, which offered round-the-clock support of the White House and absolute condemnation of critics (Greenwald and Kitty). Although amounting to only a minority of the total episodes of 2006 (roughly one-fifth), these civic-oriented episodes turned the audience from lighter entertainment and topics of primarily personal concern to something expressly public. These episodes did, however, still look and feel like *Oprah*. That is so in part because of Winfrey's adroit use of melodrama, both as rhetoric and aesthetic.

Unlike the other two talk shows we have analyzed, the *Oprah Winfrey Show*, over its twenty-two-year broadcasting history, has attracted a fair amount of scholarly interest. Livingstone and Lunt, Masciarotte, Squire, and Shattuc, all writing in the 1990s, wondered whether the show might enlarge public sphere debate, or might be feminist, especially as it gave voice to women or featured their interests and relationships to one another. The Oprah Book Club has prompted a number of scholars to write articles or full-length studies (Davis, Farr, Hall, Rooney, Striphas). Of all the studies concerning the *Oprah Winfrey Show*, those on the book club are the ones to closely consider Winfrey's verbal talents. This is especially the case with Farr and Hall, who both believe that Winfrey operates successfully as an educator during the book club episodes.

Two recent full-length studies focus on Winfrey as exemplar of cultural and historical forces (Illouz, Peck). Eva Illouz concludes her study by pointing out that Winfrey possesses an important form of knowledge: "Oprah Winfrey has known to put into ritual form the deep longing for a symbolic system that helps explain, work on, and exorcises demons of failed relationships and selfhood" (241). This is a crucial observation, and it gets at some of the reasons for the aesthetic that we will discuss below. In *The Age of Oprah*, Janice Peck, by contrast, says:

> Winfrey's rise to prominence cannot be explained solely by reference to her personal qualities or talents. That her multifaceted enterprise has resonated across an entire culture is testament to the powerful historical roots of its appeal. Winfrey's journey from talk show queen to "one of the most important figures in popular culture" must therefore be situated in relation to other developments of which it is an integral part. (6)

All of this is true, of course. But putting Winfrey at the center of a book on these "other developments" begs the question: Why Oprah? Why not someone else—or many others—who can bring together the twin ideologies of "therapy as an institution and industry" and "neoliberalism" (6–7)? As one reads along in the book, one notices that it is allegiance to these and related ideologies that explains Winfrey's success.

It is as though scholars do not know what Winfrey herself has known. The first time she hosted a talk show in Baltimore in the early 1980s, she knew her talents perfectly matched the venue. "I'm home. I'm home. I know this was what I am supposed to be doing," she has said (Koehn and Helms 3). She also knows how to choose and discipline talent to her particular creative ends:

> I could weep when I think about my team. It's all about attracting good people. I've always tried to surround myself not only with people who are smart but with people who are smarter in ways I am not. I have the best team ever. They *get* me. I feel I've created my own extended family here at work, with people who understand the code. We have a code of excellence that has been the standard bearer for us, and everybody gets it. And, if you don't get it, then you don't last very long. (9–10)

From the point of view of intentional performance, Winfrey's fingerprints are everywhere on the show. Borrowing from African American rhetoric and the New Age rhetoric that she has heavily promoted, Winfrey says that the show's "intention" is "to uplift, to enlighten, to encourage, and to entertain." This is a revision of Horace's dictum that art should delight and instruct. Winfrey's art is a popular one that delights as diverting entertainment but also partakes of something more thoroughgoing, with deeper, more disturbing, pleasures.

On the *Oprah Winfrey Show*, the audience experiences two kinds of aesthetics. On one level is a strict adherence to a bourgeois sense of taste and order. This aesthetic is evidenced in everything from the "classy" sofas—and their placement on the set—to story lines with happy endings. But on another level are aesthetic qualities that can deepen the experience of the first level, or even run counter to them. If the first level is graspable through rationality, the second always threatens to slip through that grasp. This second level is seen in the show's often lavish sensuousness, an occasional bit of carnivalesque fun, and—of the greatest importance for our analysis—an emotion-charged melodramatic aesthetic.

The effectiveness of both the rhetoric and aesthetic of the show depend upon the kind of high production values not often seen in the talk show genre, not to mention the afternoon subgenre, once the province of "trash

TV." Winfrey deliberately separated her show from that subgenre in the 1990s, lost a little in the ratings at first, but later rebounded to become the only afternoon show of that era still standing. Ever since, she has continually reinvested in the show, recently in state-of-the-art editing software (Koehn and Helms). The show can deftly imitate most other shows on television, be they evening dramas or reality television. One of the hallmarks of Winfrey's rhetorical brilliance has been her grasp of the medium of television in all its cross-generic hypermediation (Bolter and Grusin). Indeed, she understands that she is working within an almost total media environment, one that is very demanding in its round-the-clock requirements and in its constant fluidity. Her "Oprah" icon itself circulates across television programming, print, and other media to further establish the show's classiness, as well as Winfrey's ethos: someone powerful, successful, but still down-to-earth and trustworthy, someone concerned with the welfare of others, someone who (as the phrase goes) puts her money where her mouth is.

Courting the Audience Through the Fairy Tale Genre

Over the years, Winfrey moved out of the "best girlfriend" relationship with her audience (see Masciarotte and Haag)—something we might consider to be democratic—into another, which has some frankly undemocratic qualities. But in both avatars, Winfrey was courting the audience. Early on, she rushed from the stage into the studio audience with a winning smile to register their opinions before a home audience of many millions. This democratic fantasy—that women's voices matter—was celebrated by feminist scholars. But the relationship between Oprah and her audience had to undergo change. Winfrey's capitalist success increased her power and authority. What to do with such success?

In part, Winfrey used it to recraft her image such that she could herself become an A-list celebrity. At times, at least, "Oprah" is a dignified, regal, fashion plate, presiding over her own stage, yes, but also striding across the television programming into the celebrity gossip shows or other talk shows or even the evening news (as when she opened a girls' school in South Africa). There she is, as well, on the cover of her own O Magazine, but also on others; there she is on the Internet, on her own website, but elsewhere, too. There she is in name, anyway, on the cover of books that she has selected for her book club, visible prominently on the Barnes and Noble bookshelves. In the speech genre of the fairy tale, "Oprah" has metamorphosed from the ugly duckling that some in the established—white, male-owned and -managed—media originally saw into the beautiful mature swan.

Oprah's entry into posh celebrity is the apotheosis of this feminine fairy tale, just as Diana's becoming a princess was "every girl's dream." "Dreams can come true," little girls are told.

In the episodes that trade in a magical realm of female fantasy, there is no room for a dowdy Oprah to stand democratically among the audience, waiting to hear their voices. All of the space must be filled with fantasy objects. The aesthetic is upscale, never garish. All the women who appear are beautiful and flawlessly coiffed; all the men are handsome and well appointed. They are taken in hand by Oprah and led into their audience's dreams, which are simultaneously middle-class and aristocratic. When Oprah engages in the speech act of the joke with these celebrities, it is not to make an edgy or ironic statement as one might find on a late-night talk show—that is, engaging in masculine mock combat—but merely something to show the vulnerable side of powerful people, the side that will make them amenable to ordinary women's fantasies.

Some recent examples of *Oprah* fantasy shows are often, but not only, of the celebrity chat genre, which itself is transformed into something truly lavish. One recent episode took the audience on a visually lush tour of country singers Faith Hill and Tim McGraw's Tennessee home with slow pans of the pastoral scenery, as though making the audience a gift of this sensuous view. Similarly luscious looks at Hill and McGraw were on offer as the two sang a romantic duet (of course!). The stage used for the *Oprah* show is a modular one and can be completely taken apart and reformed within minutes. This occurred after the "chat" portion of the show was finished. Hill and McGraw sang as though at a cozy concert venue—perfect for a night out with a "special one." They sat facing each other on elevated perches. The background was a deep blue, and smoky—the two singers viewed through gauzy camera lenses.

"Oprah and Gayle's Big Adventure" did the same for a Thelma and Louise–like feminist imaginary: two "best friends" out on the road together, kicking back, having fun. Then there was the bra episode, which worked through a number of speech (and visual) genres: slapstick, girls' slumber party games, the genre of women's lingerie shopping, a spoof of the man-on-the-street interview, and, of course, the fashion makeover television genre. It begins with a prefilmed sequence in which two female fashion experts "attack" a woman on the street who is allegedly poorly dressed in many ways, but centrally lacks a good bra. As one of the fashion experts stands behind the woman, the other sticks her head up under the woman's blouse for a closer inspection. When the video editor returns us to the *Oprah* stage, there is Oprah, sportily dressed but with a blouse tight enough to display the result of her own well-chosen bra. She enthusiastically promises "the perfect" bra to fit each and every studio audience member who spring onto the stage. Once they do, Oprah ushers them into the "dressing room," her hands on their derriers; after they emerge, she checks out the bra fit personally.

Although it is true as others have argued that the audience is figured instrumentally as consumers—of popular music, movies, clothing—there is more to their experience than that. We would argue that the fun and sensuous nature of these shows has an important gratuitous component to it. Overtly, Winfrey urges the audience onto "their best selves," a part of the so-called American dream, the making of the self into an object of perpetual "home improvement" (see Illouz's *Oprah Winfrey and the Glamour of Misery* and *Saving the Modern Soul*). But we have suggested that in these fantasy episodes, she is also inviting them to narcissistic dreaming. Just how important this may be for anyone's psyche is worth the contemplation, but in recent years feminist scholars have often argued that it is crucial for American women (see Radway for the functions of romance in U.S. women's lives). As the argument goes, women have been held responsible for much of the culture's socializing and especially for the maintenance of the family and home environment. Add to that the fact that new media and hyperconsumerism, among a host of other cultural and economic changes, have conspired against the family as a unit, making it more and more difficult to take charge of the home. Moreover, as feminism has urged women to some version of self-realization, women with careers and children have had more than a full plate. Winfrey brings all of these concerns together and also offers an antidote: sensuous fun and fantasies. Winfrey's courtship of her audience is extravagant and well executed, with the specificity of that audience, its needs and desires, kept foremost in mind. She is both master orator and popular artist extraordinaire.

Keeping the ratings up in this fashion is no mean feat. Even in this light fantasy mode we see how well Winfrey and staff use the openness of the talk show genre and its historic connection to the variety show. Winfrey's show offers more variety than any show we can think of, drawing effectively from various television, film, and stage genres. In the case of the episodes described above, the show can move effortlessly from cozy chat to concert, from makeover television to mundane bra shopping. It is this ability to combine types and to move back and forth that is one of Winfrey's signal rhetorical and artistic achievements. But equally impressive is her understanding of the ways that an aesthetic can reach the unconscious, speaking to needs that defy articulation. Winfrey employs this knowledge to shift the purpose of the show from personal narcissism to individual even political responsibility, targeting this same group of largely middle-class white women.

Rhetoric and Melodrama

The terms *rhetoric* and *melodrama* historically denote different uses of language and gesture. Aristotle famously separated rhetoric from poetics. In what we have of the *Poetics*, he treats only drama, apparently according the highest honors to tragedy. Melodrama is often considered a modern and popular art form (Gledhill, Singer, Brooks, Williams), but it does exhibit some of the magnitude of ancient Greek tragedy, with an emphasis on spectacle and a narrative line of peaks and valleys—perhaps eliciting Aristotle's terror and pity. In any case, melodrama may be what we (post)modernists have instead of tragedy. Democracy, capitalism, and the scientific/technological revolutions have combined to present the ordinary person a paradox: more than ever power resides in the individual; more than ever it does not. Even today, third-world people are "liberated" from manual agrarian labor only to find themselves without home or livelihood. First-world college students also fear unemployment, or the cycle back to (this time, urban) manual labor in the "service sector." As Everywoman or -man scans the cosmos for a moral order in these times of rapid, extreme, and impersonal change, melodrama is there to offer some clarity, together with the necessity of emotional release. Melodramas are meant to make us jeer at the vile villains and to weep at the suffering of virtuous victim-heroes who, on the screen if nowhere else, are readily identifiable.

Aesthetics of Melodrama

Let's remind ourselves of the aesthetics of melodrama. Melodrama developed underground in eighteenth-century Europe in an environment of censorship during the rise of bourgeois sensibility (Gledhill). Its working-class themes were therefore expressed in mime to the accompaniment of music. This put special emphasis on the visual, which was only heightened when melodrama moved from stage to silent screen. Although our interest is in a television genre that is full of talk, it is worth noting that, both literally and metaphorically, melodrama lives at the edge of articulateness. It attempts to express the kind of knowledge or event that strikes us dumb. The face, the gesture, the tableaux are all as important to the aesthetic as is dialogue in communicating extremities of feeling. Moral polarities in deed and character type also communicate the same. Sometimes, as in the melodramatic films of Douglas Sirk, the set itself is hyperexpressive, stuffed with furniture and filmed in hard, bright colors that carry the heavy emotional burden also borne by the characters (Elsaesser).

But melodrama is not centered only in the static. It also excites fears and thrills, sometimes providing a rushing sensation that is imitative of the frenzied pace of modernity (Singer), which may be achieved through emotional movement alone but frequently also by means of perilous physical exertions and/or fast-cut editing. Cliffhangers are suspensions of the narrative line that dam up the audience's desire for closure. This alternation of driving movement and stasis (sometimes, as with Sirk, to the point of emotional stagnancy, according to Elsaesser) is a central feature of melodrama. Physical presence is important throughout the melodrama, whether flying around in racing cars or standing stock still, with faces and bodies contorted in expressions of grief or fear.

Altogether, melodrama offers what everyday life in the rush of modernity cannot: a form to give some shape to what is often experienced as confusing and chaotic. Brooks claims that melodrama provides explanations for the alienation and injustice that plague ordinary people in this profane age of powerful, impersonal forces (e.g., capitalism and technological advancements). Melodrama, then, perfectly suits Winfrey's purposes, as described by Illouz, as offering the audience a "moral cultural form" and a "recenter[ing of] the scattered and fragmented subjectivity of late capitalism" (238).

As may be expected, some of the wilder forms of melodrama are tamed on the Oprah Winfrey Show as it attempts a "classy"—that is, bourgeois—sensibility to match that of its largely middle-class audience. Melodrama grew up alongside realism as an aesthetic, the latter acting as standard-bearer for bourgeois values, while melodrama was free to offer the underside of realism, both in terms of working-class values as well as the nonrational content of the unconscious (Gledhill). But, as Linda Williams points out, realism and melodrama are often mutually dependent, melodrama often requiring the vehicle of realism to carry it through any given narrative. The Oprah Winfrey Show definitely offers a combination of these two aesthetics, the one representing a world that is able to be mastered through understanding, the other a world that can never be mastered at all, but rather made momentarily visible. Oprah generally tries to provide the clarity and closure of realism, but the experience of the narrative journey not only provides the thrills and emotional peaks and chasms of melodrama, it also poses problems that are ever only partially resolved. In the end, melodrama is as much about immediacy or presence as it is about ideas, even moral ones.

Melodrama was the stock-in-trade of early Oprah, where abused women, crippled children, and people with out-of-body experiences were featured guests. This species of Oprah is still available. During the same season that the civic-oriented episodes were aired, the audience was also treated to the story of a young mother, seen in grainy handheld video, racing in her car at top speed with a police car in close pursuit. The woman's car could be seen in its erratic and caroming motion, but the feeling of speed came also through the voiceover and the narrative frame. We understood from Winfrey's words that the woman had earlier warned her family of her desire to leap to her death off a particular bridge. We watched the video intently, breathlessly, waiting to discover if she would be rescued in time. She was, but just barely. An officer grabbed her arm at the same moment that her body had cleared the bridge's railing. Back in the studio, both the camera and Oprah's interviewing of the young woman, her stepdaughter, and her own mother helped to sort out the moral identifications. The close-up on another relative (stepdaughter to the suicidal woman) revealed a tearful countenance as she worried aloud about the prospect of losing her stepmom. Meanwhile, the suicidal woman's own mother was stone-faced and full of blame for her daughter. However, as the storyline disclosed the cause of the young woman's behavior to have been postpartum depression, the older woman's stoicism and stubborn refusal allied her with the villainous mental disorder. The audience may have felt (as we did) anger at the mother and sympathy for the daughter together with relief at the daughter's safety. The fear and excitement came full circle to resolve and repose due to skillful editing and dialogue.

The "old" *Oprah* was centered more onstage, with fewer prefilmed sequences, sometimes aided by still photos to illustrate what could not be seen immediately onstage. Winfrey's strong skills in a particular form of rhetoric—the melodramatic interview—were instrumental in the audience's understanding and pleasure. The interview typically begins with an introduction to the topic. Winfrey's delivery clarifies the components of the subject, introduces the characters, and limns the story line effectively. As the script moves through the melodrama, her delivery heightens tension and climax. It swells, too, with magnanimous sympathy and warmth. Although Winfrey's voice can pronounce moral judgment with careful emphasis, it can also issue forth with the calmness and wisdom of Solomon. Her delivery is marked by the kind of facial expression that is fitting for melodrama, with eyes widening in surprise or narrowing in accusation, and wide smiles or furrowed brows accompanying the script at appropriate intervals. Often, as well, she pauses to gaze out into the studio (and home) audience, eyes almost panning like a camera, to sweep them into the same emotion she is presiding over onstage: both she and the audience comprise the tableau. At other times the camera moves back in medium long shot, revealing an actor that can use her entire body in gestures to match the words she is speaking. Finally, we must not forget that

Winfrey's delivery is backed by an ethos earned as a truth teller in the revelation of her own personal difficulties. She has put herself through the same harrowing hermeneutic as her guests, discovering and revealing on-stage the "secret knowledge and hidden conflicts" (Gledhill 32) for which melodrama is famous. (Yet again, in the tradition of melodrama, much about Winfrey's private life remains veiled.) In a circular movement, her authority is granted by democratic (audience) determination. But her authority is also granted because it is aggressively taken—by a talented and dynamic personality who can fill the stage with supreme melodramatic presence.

Winfrey's brand of melodrama has usually been the kind deemed feminine, because its protagonists and audience are largely female and because it centers on domestic matters. In her study of the U.S. afternoon television talk shows of the 1980s and 1990s, Jane Shattuc makes this observation.

> Melodrama is the central precedential genre that television and film has utilized as the blueprint for the production of feminine narratives. The industrial-production process of talk shows conceives of the talk show viewer as a woman who is a mother, a homemaker, and consumer of emotion-filled narratives about socially current domestic issues. (*Talking Cure* 78)

Shattuc may see the capitalist's cynical interest in afternoon talk shows, but she also acknowledges that the audience itself may find some of its own interests represented to some degree. (What she does not seem to see, given her own industrial-sounding prose, is the creative agency of the actors onstage and the producers behind the scenes.) Gledhill points out that the nineteenth-century antecedent for today's melodrama developed what she calls a "nostalgic structure," based in

> [t]he Edenic home and family, centering on the heroine as "angel in the house" and the rural community of an earlier generation, animate images of past psychic and social well-being as "moral touchstones" against which the instabilities of capitalist expansion and retraction could be judged and in which both labourer and middle-class citizen could confront the hostilities of the modern world. (20)

As we shall see, the *Oprah Winfrey Show* is able to employ much of this structure together with its social and spiritual implications. The talk show host and her production team create a melodramatic rhetoric that runs athwart the Bush administration's masculine and masculinist rhetoric.

Rhetoric and Melodrama

In Aristotle's formulation rhetoric differed from literary art in treating not of life the universal but of the daily life of the polis—the hustle and bustle of the agora—in its specific contingencies. Rhetoric aims to move its audience not primarily to an elevated and feeling contemplation, as art would do, but to belief or action in the public sphere. For Aristotle, rhetoric was not necessarily a suspect practice. It at least had the capacity for a balance among three kinds of appeals to the audience: logos (the appeal to reason), ethos (the appeal to character, especially that of the orator's), and pathos (the appeal to emotion). Modernity has issued many challenges to Aristotle's careful ordering of this triad—logos first, pathos last—but Western rationalist ideals have often enjoyed center stage in the bourgeois public arena, until very recently. The so-called hard news of Walter Cronkite's day appealed to reason through the use of factual evidence presented in lucid, organized fashion in direct, informal prose. "The facts" were gathered by skeptical reporters who traded in literate wit and street cred, both masculine preserves. They built their ethos that way, like soldiers in a dirty war, but also relied upon the reflected avuncular authority of Cronkite, who at times, it seemed, became the voice of a nation. When he wiped a tear from his eye at the death of JFK, that was justifiable pathos.

Of the many changes that have transpired from that moment to this, one is clear: while the old rhetoric is disappearing from the mainstream view, melodrama as a mode—not always as rhetoric—has only increased its position. It holds sway on local, network and cable news, on reality television shows, in Hollywood blockbuster films and ESPN, on *People* magazine and *ET Tonight*. What used to be dismissed as a "feminine genre" can now be understood as everybody's "cultural mode," to use Linda Williams's phrase. Williams's notion is that the mode can morph, leaping from genre to genre, medium to medium; that is one reason why melodrama has cropped up everywhere. It may be well to remember, however, that rhetoric, in Plato's view, had something of the same plastic quality. A rhetorician plied the "art" of merely seeming truthful or knowledgeable on any topic whatsoever. Today's master rhetorician would do well to understand the mode of melodrama as an important contributor to the art of postmodern rhetoric, and to know how it can operate effectively within a mediated world of rapidly swirling images, propelling and propelled by virtual capitalism.

So both melodrama and rhetoric can expand, contract, transform, and move quickly, according to need. Given the highly changeable nature of modernity and contemporary popular culture, this is key. Both melodrama and rhetoric can and do involve drama and acting (in classical rhetoric, this references the fifth canon—delivery). Given the visual nature of postmodern media, rhetoric in the age of electronic, as opposed to print, media devolves to its origins as public performance, something television news was slow to learn. But the big divide between melodrama and rhetoric—that the latter is more specifically instrumental—may be bridged by Linda Williams's concept of melodrama. For her, melodrama is a dialectic between strong pathos and action. The former is what many people associate with melodrama, and, as we have said, it is gendered feminine and easily dismissed. But action, especially "prolonged climactic action," is the byword of the Hollywood blockbuster, and even includes "classic" gangster and detective films (Williams 21). It is, of course, gendered masculine, and thereby earns the kind of respect that is rarely given to the *Oprah Winfrey Show*. Nor must this action remain within the confines of fiction. Sentimental novels such as *Uncle Tom's Cabin* (treated in Williams's book) "painted metaphorical pictures of pathos and action that moved readers to strong emotion and occasionally even to action" (Williams 13). It is out of this fabric that Oprah has fashioned a new rhetoric, a form of advocacy journalism that is expressed both on the set at Harpo Studios and on location via prefilmed sequences.

The clearest brief example of Oprah's use of the melodramatic aesthetic and appropriation of journalistic conventions is illustrated in the introduction to her first "town hall" meeting, titled "Truth in America." The title evokes the show's borrowing from an actual historical practice (still alive in New England), adopted televisually by President Bill Clinton. But no generic town hall meeting begins with a melodramatic introduction, as this *Oprah* show does. The prefilmed introduction offers us a shot of Frank Rich's title *The Greatest Story Ever Sold: The Decline and Fall of the Truth* highlighted on *The New York Times* bestseller list—this is an objective, documentary genre— while a deep, pounding, suspenseful soundtrack plays in the background, the clue to a melodramatic subtext. Oprah's voiceover is simultaneously provocative and institutional, accompanied by a mix of melodramatic images and video clips that are directly related to her rhetoric: "This week, it's number 2 on *The New York Times* bestseller list. Frank Rich's new book, *The Greatest Story Ever Sold: The Decline and Fall of the Truth*, is a controversial and searing indictment of the Bush administration, challenging the reasons America went to war with Iraq." Throughout this introductory sequence, the book itself is depicted—first the front cover, then the inside pages—in a fiction of the home viewer reading Rich's book. The moving images of war and politics sandwiched between depictions of the book act as the book's coming-to-life, in the genre made famous by Disney movies of fairy tales.

These images flash by on the screen, some frozen, others highlighted by action—offered in what is clearly a television news genre. First we see a fixed image of President Bush seated at a table surrounded by his advisors, all of them dressed in formal business attire, followed by action clips of American soldiers in Iraq, running down the street, shooting their weapons at unseen enemies, while ammunition explodes in the streets of Iraq. The sounds of machine gun fire and explosions add to the drama, and the pounding music crescendos, while Oprah's voiceover continues. She seems to be reading the news: "First, Rich says, that in order to gain support for the war, the White House suggested there was connections [sic] between al-Qaeda and Saddam Hussein." A frozen shot of Bush speaking to the press is followed by photos of Osama bin Laden and Hussein, which are eventually placed side by side on the screen. Winfrey asserts: "Rich argues there was no such connections [sic]," as both images quickly vanish, replaced by an action clip of the Two Towers, fire and smoke billowing into the air. Photos of press conferences with Bush, who appears smiling and relaxed, follow, while Winfrey states, "Next, Rich takes the news media to task for not asking the hard questions in the aftermath of 9/11, even criticizing his own paper, *The New York Times*. And finally," Oprah's voice continues, as the images blur in the background and the white, shadow words, "24/7," "Infotainment," and "Critical Thinking" all slowly flash across and then fade from the screen, "Frank Rich argues that our overheated, 24/7 infotainment culture, from cable news to the tabloids, has conditioned us to stop engaging in critical thinking. This is what he says."

More action-packed images of war and destruction follow, with American soldiers running for their lives as explosions occur all around them and Winfrey finishes: "According to Frank Rich, in this environment, where he says drama counts more than judicious journalism, the line between truth and fiction becomes blurred and that has made us a society that rarely questions what we are told and a society that is easily manipulated." During this final piece, stills of the provoking "Mission Accomplished" sign and Jessica Lynch are followed with more shadow words that flash and fade across the screen: "Truth," "Rarely Questions," and "Easily Manipulated."

This particular excerpt is intriguing for a variety of reasons. First, it reflects the high quality of production that has become commonplace on the *Oprah Winfrey Show* and that helps to set it apart from other daytime talk shows. Second, it illustrates Winfrey's use of rational "hard" news generic conventions like an institutional tone and news footage of actual events, while remaining situated squarely within the sensational—but masculine—melodramatic aesthetic (swelling music, explosions, gunfire, and the pastiche of provocative images and words flashing and fading across the screen with dramatic speed). Finally, in spite of her skeptical institutional tone and careful language, Winfrey clearly intends this piece to be persuasive. While she *says* "Frank Rich argues" and "[a]ccording to Rich," emulating the language and tone of objectivity one might hear from more "serious" or "hard" news sources, the melodramatic *images* that flash across the screen actually reinforce all of the claims that Winfrey attributes to Rich, belying this supposed neutrality and revealing the speech genre's persuasive intent.

This rhetoric also proposes action. The Rich episode is one of *Oprah*'s town hall programs that invites the studio audience to ask questions. Here we are back to the site of the talk show, in the studio, with cameras and microphones trained on the stage and on the studio audience. The televisual "town hall" is cross-generic with the kind of afternoon talk show that Winfrey first mastered, but Winfrey is a more formal host here, as formal as if she were hosting a presidential debate. The studio audience questioners seem to have been chosen before filming, for they leap up with alacrity, one at a time, before a roving microphone. Nonetheless, the questions seem genuine, and a dialogue between the audience member and Rich—initiated and mediated by Winfrey—does occur. Here is an example of the first exchange between the audience and guest. The genre seems to us to be taken as much from classroom rhetoric—with Winfrey as teacher—as the town hall genre, where citizens can directly challenge elected officials. We reproduce the whole to preserve its dialogic quality.

Winfrey: Who here believes that we were not deliberately lied to [by the Bush administration about the reasons for going to war in Iraq]? Not? Yes? Hi.

Unidentified Woman #5: I don't believe we were deliberately lied to. And if you look at the history in regards to all the intelligence, not only did President Bush get the same intelligence, but so did President Clinton. And the bottom line is this: Saddam Hussein himself could have stopped this war. He did not comply with the UN. He did not comply with the weapons inspectors. What else were we to do as a nation?

Rich: Well, according to the Hans Blix report, Saddam was cooperating and what Blix told the UN was, "just give us a few more months. He's now opening up the sites to us. Let us go in." For whatever reason, we called it back and ended it, and ended that containment. On your first point, there was some intelligence that was good.

Woman #5: Right.

Rich: There was some intelligence saying there was no connection with 9/11. I guess the issue is, is it enough to go to war with Saddam if he wasn't planning to send a mushroom cloud our way? That's something you could debate. Take him out 'cause he's a horrible guy, a terrible dictator.

Woman #5: Right. Which he was.

Rich: That—which he definitely was. A horrible person in history.

Woman #5: Right.

Rich: But that wasn't the reason they gave us. That's the reason they talk about now. But before the war, it was all, a smoking gun will be a mushroom cloud, there could be a nuclear bomb in a major city. And there was no evidence to support that.

Woman #5: Did someone from the Bush administration directly say that Iraq was a link?

Rich: I'll let you be the judge. They never said Saddam Hussein ordered the attacks of 9/11.

Woman #5: Right.

Rich: Absolutely they never said that. But Dick Cheney, for instance, repeatedly said, "We know Mohamed Atta met with intelligence agents from the Saddam Hussein regime in the months before 9/11 in Prague." That meeting never happened.

Woman #5: Suggested that, yeah.

Rich: So it's the power of suggestion. So . . .

Winfrey: Well, let's ask this audience—let's ask this audience, before we went to war, were you under the impression that Saddam Hussein and Iraq had something to do with 9/11? Were you? Were you not? You did not think so? [pointing at an audience member] . . . Yes, ma'am, you wanted to raise your hand? Hi.

Unidentified Woman #6: I would like to say that one of the clearest ways to get your message through and be credible is by not saying it. It's by innuendo, it's by implication, it's by mindwashing.

The dialogue moves quickly because the show's production keeps the transitions between segments and speakers seamless, and yet, there is just enough questioning and hesitation (note Winfrey's questions before alighting on woman #6) to maintain the feel of spontaneity. Even though these questioners were almost certainly chosen before the show, the speakers do appear to be using their own language, and genuinely interacting with the guest and Winfrey. This is important, and less because of the treatment of the studio audience than that of the home audience, for they are being symbolically invoked. We in the home audience are treated to a dialogue that is rarely offered on any popular television show. Perhaps the reason that Winfrey has the courage to offer such fare—and during the "frivolous" afternoon hours, no less—is that she has a historic connection with her audience. She understands that they want to be entertained, but she also seems to believe that they would like to be addressed as thinking adults. On this day, the home audience is meant to understand that they, too, are invited to be assertive, questioning citizens—within very definite bounds of civility (and the bounds of television production), enforced onstage by Winfrey herself. Whether the audience is invited to question Winfrey and the melodramatic production of her television program is left unaddressed, however.

From Angel in the House to Angel Network

The masculine has enjoyed a longer presence in the public sphere and can be well represented in both melodrama and rhetoric; the feminine has been obliged to invent and adapt. In the West, women began to enter the public sphere in large numbers in the nineteenth century, and as they did so, they brought with them the values associated with that "other" sphere. We have already discussed the introduction to the study by Christine Gledhill that helped to usher in contemporary melodrama studies, but we return to it now to remind ourselves of the history of melodrama, especially its feminine characteristics.

> [M]elodrama's challenge lies not in confronting how things are, but rather in asserting how they ought to be. But since it operates within the frameworks of the present social order, melodrama conceives "the promise of human life" not as a revolutionary future, but rather as a return to a "golden past": less how things ought to be than how they should have been. The Edenic home and family, centering on the heroine as "angel in the house" and the rural community of an earlier generation, animate images of past psychic and social well-being as "moral touchstones" against which the instabilities of capitalist expansion and retraction could be judged and in which both labourer and middle-class citizen could confront the hostilities of the modern world. (21)

In almost every way, this quotation suits *Oprah*. The "family" on the *Oprah Winfrey Show* is complex and postmodern, but it functions also as a "moral touchtone." There are times on the show when one wonders whether the "golden past" on *Oprah* might be the 1960s of U.S. history. Quite obviously, the "angel in the house" morphs into the cyborgian woman who logs onto Oprah's Angel Network website and uses her credit card to donate "an end table" (actually suggested on the site) to victims of Hurricane Katrina. Because the politics of the *Oprah Winfrey Show* are patently not "revolutionary," but mildly reformist, Winfrey will at times hide behind the vagueness of a golden past to avoid direct confrontations with powerful others, or even with the source of her own capitalist power. But though the *Oprah Winfrey Show* moves through Gledhill's melodramatic tradition, Winfrey does ultimately create out of it a melodramatic rhetoric of action in the present moment.

It begins by constituting a new postmodern space for the rhetorician as family member. We can see this at work in the episode "Living on the Minimum Wage," featuring guest Morgan Spurlock and his wife Alex, who also appears as his latter-day hippie, vegan girlfriend in his film *Supersize Me*, a kind of experiential expose of the risks to health posed by eating fast food. Spurlock now has a reality show on the cable channel FX that claims to document thirty days in the life of a person who agrees to live in a radically new social environment (i.e., a white bigot living with a black family); it is a show with definite liberal political overtones. On this *Oprah* episode, Spurlock and Alex agree to live for a month on minimum wage jobs.

The minimum wage program features talk with Spurlock, Alex, and Winfrey onstage before the studio audience in a genre that transforms celebrity chat by its invocation of serious issues—that is, the "chat" genre is in Bakhtinian dialogue with news and other factual or realist rhetoric. The traditional talk show portion of the program is interwoven with prefilmed segments that mimic the kind of reality television Spurlock produces for FX. Moving back and forth between the two, Winfrey is able to question the guests and to emphasize key moments of experiential logos—the primary form of knowledge that the show offers, other than a few facts proffered in the opening news-genre monologue—and pathos from the filmed narrative. The whole builds an ethos of sincerity and concern on the part of both Winfrey and guests. These are modernist elements that comport well with the use of journalistic and documentary realism and their usual focus on stable "true" realities. The modern news and realist genres are put into dialogue with the postmodern reality television genre, creating a program that is another dialogic genre, a combination of Spurlock's *30 Days* (itself quite hybridized or dialogized) and *Oprah*. Winfrey has combined on her own show some trendy variety together with substantive "content" (as the media executives refer to it) at relatively little expense. She adapts Spurlock's show to the needs of her audience through framing devices, interrogative dialogue, and the addition of the coffee-klatsch intimacy of Winfrey in the onstage "live" portion of the program. Finally, she has simultaneously promoted a show she presumably believes in that has lower ratings than hers.

Time and again the new *Oprah* creates a space of celebrity "family" that is promotional of a particular political idea or charity, of the specific celebrities and their products (recent films or CDs they have made), and of Winfrey and all of her products. But Winfrey is clearly the head of this capitalist and virtual family, and in this position she often revises the role of rhetorician to fit her feminine body. Time and again Winfrey reinvents herself onstage or in a prefilmed sequence as someone with authority who more or less governs the proceedings. Winfrey's privileged behind-the-scenes knowledge of the Spurlock film boosts her authoritative ethos as talk show host and news-magazine anchor. On the global warming episode, Winfrey sits stationary on a stool while Al Gore strides the stage during and between video clips of his film *An Inconvenient Truth*. Again she poses questions, but this time it is as though she is the professor hosting a guest lecturer. For the Hurricanes Katrina and Rita episodes, she is the "on location" news anchor, with celebrities like Julia Roberts and real CNN reporters Lisa Ling and Anderson Cooper acting as her correspondents. Nor does she forget her own television roots, we might say. She often positions herself as "girlfriend"—to take a term from Masciarotte (this is, after all, not a biological family—Winfrey herself is not even married). After Spurlock "confesses" (on the "Confession Camera") that he went hungry trying to live on the minimum wage, Winfrey responds naively: "Wow! I never thought of that." In this manner, she continues to court her audience, while offering them honorary membership in her "family" of mostly celebrities, but occasionally also of intellectuals and artists (most especially in the book club episodes of recent years), liberal activists (like Spurlock), philanthropists, and liberal politicians.

The audience is also directly addressed on *Oprah* as mothers and daughters who are still subject to "the hostilities of the modern world," but who, on the new *Oprah*, are increasingly positioned as women of some privilege. At the beginning of the minimum wage show, the audience sees Winfrey first, dressed conservatively in dark colors, in medium shot with a video screen behind and to her right that projects the title of today's show. She looks into the camera and delivers the introduction. We will join midparagraph.

That's $8,000 less than what our government even considers poverty. The truth is that one out of every four workers earns even less than $8.70 an hour. Could you raise your children on that? Well, millions of people are. And why should you care? Because they are the very people that we all rely on each and every day. They are teacher's aides in your children's classroom, they are caring for your aging parents in a nursing home, they make sure that your hotel runs and your offices and schools are clean, security guards keeping buildings safe, paramedics who are there in your most desperate hour. So our goal today is to open your eyes and hopefully your hearts to the millions of people around us who work thankless jobs for very little pay.

Early on melodrama is implicit and/or lightly offered by means of intensifying words and Winfrey's own dramatic delivery ("what our *government even* considers poverty"). It then opens up with a long, five-clause compound sentence—the kind only spoken in conversation by someone who is passionate—and ends on an obviously melodramatic note of imagined suffering ("paramedics, who are there in your most *desperate* hour" [emphasis Winfrey's]). The explicit advocacy of the working poor, not something that television journalists sworn to objectivity are generally allowed to include in a news story even in these postmodern times, is the mark of Winfrey's new intimacy with her audience. Winfrey, who has shared personal heartache, bra style, and "my favorite things" with her audience, now shares her "goal" with them: "to open your eyes and hopefully your hearts."

That the latter suggests audience action (digging into their pocketbooks and remembering social issues in the voting booth) can be deduced from a number of contextual clues. Viewers can at any time donate to the Angel Network, her charity organization (also linked to Oprah's website and mentioned in her magazine, O: *The Oprah Magazine*); the audience was explicitly asked to do so during the shows on Hurricanes Katrina and Rita. Viewers are invoked as voters when the show features liberal political guests (and increasingly the balance is in favor of liberals). A number of such guests appeared before the upcoming midterm election: Al Gore, Barack Obama, *New York Times* political reporter Frank Rich, political commentator Bill O'Reilly, and New Orleans mayor Ray Nagin. Winfrey herself has finally made it clear whom she supports for president. She adds this explicit political action to her already-established philanthropic activities, for which she not only donates her own funds, but consciously acts as a role model before her viewers. Many of the celebrities who appear on her show are also positioned as philanthropic role models. Later in the program on the minimum wage, the invoking of the audience to action is continued by Spurlock's wife Alex, tearful over the generosity of a church organization in a poor neighborhood: "They have nothing and they give everything away that they have." This is a speech genre that can be feminine, traced to the "tear-jerker" films of the past. But it is also in dialogue with those from inspirational movies of the past, especially from the 1930s and 1940s (still seen on television), depicting orphans, hobos, and decent ordinary (yet heroic) men (played by James Stewart or Gary Cooper).

On 6 September 2005, *Oprah* aired a program titled "Oprah on Location: Inside the Katrina Catastrophe." In this episode, she interviews New Orleans Mayor Ray Nagin on the street in front of the Hyatt Hotel in New Orleans in the days following the hurricane and evacuation of hundreds of thousands of New Orleans residents. He describes the horrific conditions experienced by Katrina survivors during the five days they spent inside the Superdome awaiting federal intervention in the way of essential resources like water and food, and recounts examples of various atrocities experienced by women and children victims during this time, such as rape and murder. After Nagin becomes visibly choked up and walks away from the interview, Winfrey faces first her crew and then looks directly into the camera, declaring through tears as she stamps her feet and waves a fist in the air, "This makes me so mad! This makes me so mad. This should not have happened. This should not have happened." What might read as a stunt on another program on *Oprah* does not, owing to her long-term relationship with her audience and to her accumulated ethos. This she has achieved on these now-numerous civic-oriented *Oprah* episodes, but also on such showy episodes as the one where she calls the memoirist James Frey a liar, and through the public relations of her philanthropy work. Her ethos while uttering this genre of moral outrage is secure.

The melodramatic mode, too, saves her from appearing to be politically biased. Winfrey does not attempt to lay blame at the feet of any particular individual or institution, instead focusing on *how things should have been*; she is clear in articulating the tragedy through the lens of moral responsibility, and in delivering a synergistic appeal to her predominately middle-class female audience to help her set things to right. She begins and ends in the space of innocence, portraying Katrina survivors as "virtuous victims" and the bureaucrats who prevented them from receiving timely assistance as the potential villains of this particular melodrama, while managing to distance herself from a political position that would alienate members of her audience who consider themselves politically conservative. There are veiled references to "the feds" and to the lack of response as being "about politics," but Winfrey is careful to avoid a specific political affiliation or clear accusations against specific persons or entities.

Further, rather than emphasizing the potential role of race or class in the lack of prompt federal response, Winfrey encourages others, like Nagin, to broach the issue, allowing her to appear to inhabit a neutral, objective position that enhances her ethos. W. Lance Bennett points out that "[j]ournalists play their gatekeeper role (or, if you prefer, exercise their power) in a low-key way that seems to avoid taking sides" (15), and Winfrey's approach in these episodes reflects her awareness of the idealized role the American journalist is supposed to play under such circumstances. She is no stranger to the conventions of news: she was a ten-year veteran of local television news when she took over as anchor for *A.M. Chicago*, the program that eventually became nationally syndicated as the *Oprah Winfrey Show*. A former black beauty queen who was often disparaged for her looks on white-owned television shows (Manga 28), she also knows the limits of objectivity. It would be difficult, indeed, to believe that she does not know how her black female body "reads" to her mainstream audience, nor how Nagin's would. Here is a visual version of ethos. That it should go unheralded does lend an added gravitas.

Communications scholar Corner is interested in the hybridization of news, "the mixing of elements from what were previously distinct conventions, thus breaking down some of the older genres, including those dividing 'higher' from 'lower' forms or demarcating the 'serious' from the 'entertaining'" (28). Certainly the new *Oprah* shows demonstrate this. On the episode aired on the Katrina disaster, for instance, the program opens, not within the traditional studio set employed by the *Oprah Winfrey Show*, but with a head-and-shoulders shot of Winfrey seated at a desk, directly addressing her viewing audience. Her hair is pulled back tightly, and she is wearing a conservative, button-down, pale blue blouse. Behind her is a backdrop of a shot of post-Katrina New Orleans, where she is clearly on location. News anchor Winfrey uses the serious tone and reporting style of the evening news: "With the city underwater and under siege, we found Mayor Ray Nagin, who refused to evacuate." The cameras cut immediately to an excerpt providing graphic images of the catastrophic destruction of downtown New Orleans, complete with melodramatic background music, and Winfrey, performing as both news anchor and reporter, narrates as the footage plays. The speech genre is an interplay of genres from investigative reporting but also from the masculine melodrama of the hard-boiled detective novel (and the like): "All week long, Mayor Ray Nagin never left his city. I found him at his command post, at the Hyatt Hotel." What follows is the prerecorded interview footage mentioned above, originally filmed using handheld cameras, a move which simultaneously reinforces Winfrey's ethos and pathos: the sense of immediacy transmitted by footage that appears to be less edited and produced than the excerpts it is sandwiched between. The use of text at the bottom of the screen—"Oprah: Live on Location in New Orleans"—appears throughout the program; that, and the institutional manner in which the footage is introduced, mimic the conventions of "hard" or "serious" news sources, which lends the episode the ethos that is both consciously and unconsciously associated with hard news, while simultaneously blurring the boundaries between the "serious" and the "entertaining." The dramatic interview with Nagin, during which both he and Winfrey are moved to tears and anger over the unnecessary suffering of the hurricane victims, makes a candid appeal to the viewer's emotions.

Artistically, the *Oprah Winfrey Show* is innovative throughout these civic-oriented episodes. Indeed, the show may be producing a new type of melodrama, one that links it to the functions of news rhetoric without losing the pathetic depths of the mode. In it, the presence of the speaker—in this case, the host of the show—is supplemented most often by the documentary camera. This is a form of melodrama in which the images move at the pace of the descriptive and expository speech, alternating understanding and emotion. In one of the Hurricane Rita and Katrina episodes, the images illustrate the words as, or just after, they are spoken. A hurricane victim says, "There are no businesses open," while we see an image first of a business pre-flood, then a picture of the same place, ruined (from virtually the same camera angle). This occurs several times throughout the narrative featuring the middle-class white woman who tours the neighborhood in a car and on foot with Lisa Ling. Then, in a kind of flashback—to illustrate another part of her conversation with Ling—the woman returns to her home with her family, her husband and two children, while she speaks of worries about her children encountering contaminated water. What would be an ordinary, but serious, conversation is belied by the reality all around. The ordinary conversation is like a photograph; the scene around the speakers is like a negative of the same photograph. The overall aesthetic, then, is a blend of the real and surreal, the handheld camera operating in exceptionally harsh light: "This is your home?"/"This is my home" (we see a glaringly white concrete foundation festooned with rubble). Music is minimal but when present, low and foreboding. At one point a dog is seen amid wreckage, sitting still until suddenly coming to life and barking. A rare television silence accompanies stills or moving images of people's homes or even bodies. One almost seems to hear an eerie wind whistling in accompaniment. The didacticism of the speech/visual illustration contributes to the rational bourgeois intelligibility, while some of the content of the speech, the close-ups of teary-eyed or stunned victims, and the landscape pans all express devastating loss, both seen and not seen through the harsh glare of the lighting.

Rhetorically, these episodes combine feminine and masculine melodramatic rhetoric in a female address that moves the site of conflict from the home and the individual psyche to a realm that is explicitly social and political. Yes, Oprah Winfrey does endorse products and engage in splashy giveaways. Her programs do contain plenty of commercials. Harpo Productions does charge television stations top dollar to air her syndicated show (Koehn and Helms 8). But an analysis that sees this and not the arguably ethical goals of these civic-oriented episodes is missing part of the picture. Indeed, the distance between the rich and the poor is sometimes thematized directly, including in the episodes on Hurricanes Katrina and Rita. Shiny new FEMA trailers are repeatedly juxtaposed with muddy tents. Winfrey sometimes speaks, apparently frankly, about what it means to be successful—in American terms—and to have a conscience.

The Angel Network, according to *Oprah's* website, has raised more than $50 million since its inception in 1998 in its efforts to "help underserved people rise to their own potential" (oprah.com). The network provides funds for scholarships to Boys and Girls Clubs of America, to Habitat for Humanity (which builds homes for the poor), to build schools in rural areas in ten different countries, and to help provide food, clothes, and education to children in South Africa, among many others. Winfrey reinforces her already well-established ethos through her own personal philanthropy—by paying 100 percent of the operating and fundraising costs out of her own pocket for the network, her viewers can be assured that their entire donation will be used for charitable purposes (oprah.com). We should observe, in the body of our text rather than in a footnote, that Oprah's Angel Network has received the highest rating possible by Charity Navigator, an organization that examines the forms that charities use to report their income to the government.

Although the immediate goal in some of these *Oprah* shows may be to persuade the viewer to purchase an end table for a hurricane victim, these episodes may well have had more influence than that. They seem to have been part of a new liberal movement in U.S. politics, the most obvious manifestation of which was to win Barack Obama the presidency. We may recall that *The Global Village Revisited* considers the hosts of the talk shows under analysis to be "good" orators. Certainly, we can say that Winfrey is a talented and effective orator who intends to do good as well. In the end, it is impossible to know how or whether the new *Oprah* does more harm than good in its inculcation of a fantasy and consumerist ethos side by side with that of a virtual "caring" family—a family headed by adults (both women and men), disciplined to vote and perform good deeds. This citizen-family exists in a world that is both revealed and obscured through melodrama. Not only is it difficult to know whether the overall rhetoric of the new *Oprah* is good or bad; it is difficult to know how a melodramatic rhetoric will (as Williams puts it) leap from one locale to the next and morph into its political opposite. And considering the vagaries of politics, it is hard to know how anybody's rhetoric will figure in the larger picture. What we do see is that, given the right conditions and the resources—including, in this case, a talent for melodramatic rhetoric—the public sphere is capable of some kind of reconstitution. The show provides firm evidence that such a thing is indeed occurring.

CHAPTER FIVE

~

Conclusion

Each of these case studies seems to be its own world, incommensurable. This might come as a surprise, particularly as the concept of global imperialism has been an influential one. McLuhan's own notion of the global village, while still a fitting metaphor for one of the effects of watching television, cannot, however, be used here as an emblem of the kind of understanding we hope our case studies have fostered. Cosmopolitanism has recently emerged as a descriptor for one who considers herself a citizen of the world. However, it is a term that so far has been mainly addressed to elites. It is also still somewhat inchoate: "We are not exactly certain what it is, and figuring out why this is so and what cosmopolitanism may be raises difficult conceptual issues. As a practice, too, cosmopolitanism is yet to come, something awaiting realization" (Pollack et al., 1). Nationalism has still seemed a better means of binding the individual cases and of making the comparisons across them.

Showto Na Slavi

Even considering the critiques of nationalism as a hegemonic and brutally unifying force, it would be easy to celebrate the attempts by *Showto Na Slavi* to forge a new Bulgarian identity. As R. J. Crampton put it recently, "Bulgaria's record for the treatment of minorities is generally an impressive one" (*Aleksandur Stamboliiski* 20). And although nationalism frequently rears its ugly head in the region, the Balkan Wars do seem long over for Bulgaria. The country and most of the people seem focused on survival. Indeed, it appears that the nationalistic and imperialistic aggression of other larger countries like Russia, England, Germany, and the United States (to name some of the most recent actors) have had an enormous impact on Bulgaria's fortunes. It would be easy, therefore, for first-world scholars especially to take a reflexive, paternalistic approach to the interpretation of Bulgarian popular culture.

Certainly we must acknowledge *Showto Na Slavi*'s relatively benign nationalism. A Bulgarian English professor and translator who had previously worked with Trifonov told us that the troupe was trying to make up for the fact that the state was unable to provide education to young people at the level enjoyed under Communism. It is in order to repair and even build anew that the show exhibits unifying elements that would not be seen on the *Tonight Show*, for example. That a late-night talk show would unfold its first half in an uninterrupted twenty-minute thematically unified sketch, rather than a collection of unrelated jokes and celebrity interviews, is noteworthy. That it might take part in some kind of educational or communal enterprise is stunning. The explicit foregrounding of not only Bulgarian themes, but also enactments of Bulgarian community suggests that the show has a project, a forger of a "vox populi" not only for the Slavi troupe but for the audience itself. *Showto Na Slavi* moves backward and forward through time, reminding viewers of what they share, healing their wounds, stoking their historical imaginations, and inviting them loudly back to the public stage. Our analysis of the speech genres of one episode—not an atypical one in 2003—show that rituals, proverbs, and even satire often work to these ends.

But there is more to the political aesthetic than that of a unifying and wholesome revision of the late-night talk show genre. The first half of the show is brash and anarchic, even as it converges toward a center. Its satire of Bulgarian politics is wickedly sharp, so much so that it is not clear from which perspective the satire proceeds. Sometimes it seems as if all government were equally suspect, that all government is as disreputable as the former Communist one or the many succeeding corrupt ones. Indeed, a Ukrainian linguist who heard one of our presentations on *Slavi* expressed surprise that as late as 2003, more than a decade after the fall of Communism, the show was still skewering it. If one aim of the show is to help rebuild the Bulgarian citizen, it is also the case that much in the satire especially suggests that government (not just Simeon's government) is ridiculous and highly suspect. In our episode, the Slavi troupe joins with the audience in reenacting the Communist brigadier movement. The satiric sketch brings Bulgarians together through the sense of shared hardship and past oppression and probably reminds them of continuing oppression carried out by a more vaguely configured overlord. However, it is also the case that Bulgarians are being brought together as outsiders and naysayers, creative and energetic though they are.

As the clashing colors and genres are tossed together, confusion arises. Some of the confusion is probably expressive of bewilderment at Bulgarians' current predicament. But some may be a productive chaos that could and should involve us all at a very deep human level. *Showto Na Slavi* is an unusually sensuous talk show, full of music, motion, and myth. In the first half, *Slavi* is devoted to motion in the form of hyperbolic language and physical gestures (including dance), not to mention a *mise en scene* full of eye-popping colors. Slavi sometimes portrays himself as a Turk, bending over for gay sex, or as the husband of Temenushka, the oversexed village wife. During the interview with Georgi the Formula One driver, Slavi says he feels like the wolf in the Russian cartoon *Nu, Pogodi* as he lowers his large frame into the small car. The wolf is analogous to Wile E. Coyote in the U.S. Warner Brothers cartoon *Road Runner*. Both are truncated forms of the trickster figure that Paul Radin limns.

Slavi is not "politically correct" in the Western sense, but surely a democratic politics must include a space for the trickster, the carnival, the embodied spirituality of Gellner's "local culture," which preceded nationalism. In its (modern and Western-determined) "backwardness," Bulgaria still seems to enjoy something of its peasant past, which extended into the Communist period and probably lives still, though in an altered form. We think that it lived on *Showto Na Slavi* as late as 2003. We feel fortunate to have come across it, and we offer its indomitable and joyous spirit to our readers as well. This is not to say that the show should be seen as a model for a political platform on feminism or Turkish or gay minority rights. The carnival and mythic registers are political in the sense of being broadly democratic, not specifically so. They bring us all together in our common human destiny. It is not often that television programming, especially with its new emphasis on targeting niche audiences, can or will offer such essential human nourishment. In that regard, "poor" Bulgarians may be the richer ones.

In any case, the overall political aesthetic on *Slavi*, we would have to say, is a paradoxical one. Its parts are balanced and complementary, but also volatile and contradictory. The "centrifugal" forces are nearly as strong as the "centripetal" ones (Bakhtin, "Discourse" 272–73). Furthermore, of our three shows, *Showto Na Slavi* is the one to move to the outer edge of "someone else's" language. About one-third of its interview guests are non-Bulgarian, and require actual translators to communicate. There is another exocentric aspect to *Slavi*. The cocreator of the show, Lyuben Dilov Jr., as well as the *Showto Na Slavi* website in 2003, emphasized the show's genesis from the *Tonight Show with Jay Leno*, perhaps as a means of "selling" it in a world where "class" television might seem to come from the United States. Indeed, cocreator Lyuben Dilov Jr. presented himself to us as a vigorous and articulate salesman.

In a variety of ways, Bulgarians are encouraged to think of themselves within an international framework without losing track of themselves as Bulgarians—or indeed, as Balkan peoples, or Slavs (Serbia and Russia being frequently mentioned on the show). Bulgaria is not and probably never could have been "the Belgium of the Balkans" (Crampton, *Aleksandur Stamboliiski* 25) as Konstantin Stoilov, the prime minister of Bulgaria at the end of the nineteenth century, had hoped. To be sure, this is what many contemporary Bulgarian intellectuals might still desire. Nor is Bulgaria any longer capable of being the enlightened and democratic peasant nation that Alexander Stamboliiski envisioned in the early twentieth century. There are many fewer Bulgarian villagers. Young people flock to the cities or emigrate abroad, creating a diasporic "Bulgaria" that attracts online viewers of *Showto Na Slavi*. Bulgaria's uncertain present has been ably and artistically represented, and perhaps partially shaped, by *Showto Na Slavi*, which imagines a future for Bulgaria that is still mindful of the past.

Jan Publiek

From its inception, *Jan Publiek* was a show created from the idea that looking outward—to the Netherlands, to England, to the United States, and to commercial media in general—might in fact result in an audience discussion show format that would enable the program to compete for audience share with its commercially produced competitors, and also entice the usually reserved "ordinary" Flemings to loquacity. Whether Jan Van Rompaey was correct in his initial assumption we cannot say, but it is certainly the case that awkward silence was not a key feature of the program, not even during the first full-fledged season airing in 1997. The light, popular-culture topics favored on most of the episodes may have encouraged panelist speech but they assuredly matched the tone and speech genres in which the host himself excelled. The large number of panelists together with invited guests plus the desire on the part of the host to give all speakers a chance to hold the floor placed a heavy requirement on cogency. The host's role on *Jan Publiek* also required him to use his talent for witty repartee. Thus the speech genres favored on the show were short and dialogic. Some speakers were better at this than others.

We have said that the political aesthetic of *Jan Publiek* brought together the classical notions of balance and symmetry with the politics of egalitarianism and public civility. This seems true even though the show was fairly host-centered. A few panelists on the program developed distinctive characters that the audience enjoyed, characters that were made intelligible through the comic framing of the show by the host and producers—and in the end, also ratified by some of the panelists and the audience. This added another requirement on the speakers to maintain a light, genial tone, employing the speech genres to match. Again, some panelists were better able to produce these qualities than were others. In general, the more conversational, easy-going utterances and dialogues seemed to create the personas that audiences appreciated most. Van Rompaey brought to the show not only his talent of quick wit and his many years of proven abilities as a popular feature journalist and entertainer, he also imposed order on the proceedings and helped to establish a slightly aristocratic bearing to what would otherwise be a very populist and at times commercial rhetoric. Indeed, although the symmetry and order are striking, the fact that the show could accommodate such different personas as Rudi, Simone, and Betty should argue a firm place for *Jan Publiek* in the history of the civic-oriented talk show.

However, the show could not accommodate everyone equally. This should be expected for a number of reasons. First, the notion of equality is itself problematic. If to be treated equally means to be treated the same, how ought, for example, pregnant women be treated in the workplace? Gender, as theorist Judith Butler (and others) have shown, is a tenacious feature of human life that is, if anything, confirmed by the recent transgender movement within which biological "women" do sometimes become biological "men," and vice versa. Other poststructuralist philosophers have made the case that difference is what makes meaning possible; women are women because men need to define themselves against them. Finally, the postmodern philosopher Jean Baudrillard argued that difference was exactly what the new world of the mass-mediated image was stealing from us. Whatever virtue equality names, it cannot be the means of effacing difference. We will return to this theme.

This book also makes the case that a revival of aesthetic appreciation of even commercial television can lead us to new insights. One of the things that we first noted with regard to *Jan Publiek*, but which is true of all talk shows, is that talent matters. Each of our programs seems to have its own rhetorical requirements. One reason for the lack of equality among the panelists on *Jan Publiek* is simply that some were better speakers than others, particularly with regard to this format and to the overall political aesthetic, which was obviously reflective of mainstream, bourgeois values. The panelist Damien seemed unable to communicate well within the show's particular dialogic format and overall political aesthetic. Possibly he was not a good speaker in any environment or not a good performer before the camera. But it may also be that his political aesthetic was a mismatch for that of *Jan Publiek.*

This brings us back to the discussion of difference with regard to the political aesthetic. The "Migrant Riots" episode itself marked a difference with what had been *Jan Publiek's* light and balanced qualities. Our analysis of this episode shows it to be at least partly intelligible within the mode of melodrama. When Rudi referred to Arab merchants or when the Muslim woman activist came back at Rudi with the "stupid Belgian" retort, it is hard to know whether we have racism or nationalism at work, but we do certainly have the villains and victims associated with melodrama. This episode, which finally required the panelists to weigh in on something of serious civic importance, might have been better handled had the producers considered the prospect of a melodramatic political aesthetic. The show's democratic genius might have shone had there been greater possibilities for exchange across the lines of native Flemish and immigrant difference. An interesting point: Muslim immigrants can become Belgian but cannot become Flemish, as Flanders is not a nation. Nonetheless, as Alexander Dhoest makes clear, "cultural nationalism" can be a powerful force. It may not be only in "America" that "melodrama takes on enormous importance as the engine of legitimacy for racially constituted groups whose very claim to citizenship lies in these spectacles of pathos and action" (Williams 44).

The *Oprah Winfrey Show*

At first glance, the *Oprah Winfrey Show* does not seem to circumscribe a national meaning. It is a show that has outlived its competition by staying in close and dialogical relationship with only a portion of the U.S. citizenry through its largely middle-class female audience. It maintains a rich "classy" aesthetic to pamper the frantic housewife and working woman, treating her to adventurous and romantic experiences that elevate her above the daily grind. The production values are so high that Winfrey can pretend to be a part of an evening dramedy like *Desperate Housewives* without injury to the show's typical aesthetic. The number of speech genres from which the show may choose is dizzyingly large. The show draws from genres that range across several media, including dramatic and documentary film, television variety show and comedy, and women's self-help magazines and books. The particular speech genres featured on the show are enormously various, but the show's ethic and aesthetic remains firmly grounded in middle-class feminine values and a centrist political perspective. The audience is thereby simultaneously comforted, educated, and delighted.

However, out of this grounding the host and creative team have embarked on a larger mission: to persuade middle-class women that those outside of the mainstream ought to be included in the American "family," and that said family ought to be a more responsible, communal entity, rather than merely a collection of individuals. In 2006, the show featured a number of programs that were not, strictly speaking, entertaining. The show borrowed from documentary, journalistic, reality television, and town hall genres to educate the audience in what were mainly U.S. liberal political values, values that had been harshly disparaged and decentered by media-literate right-wing ideologues during the Bush administration. Mass media orator extraordinaire Oprah Winfrey undertook to persuade her mainstream female audience to have a heart for those less fortunate: minimum wage workers, the victims of Hurricanes Rita and Katrina, and the earth (global warming). Sometimes, the audience (and Winfrey) were portrayed as victims of the right-wing march to war in Iraq. Orator Winfrey carefully balanced the roles of victim and hero(ine), as she also carefully balanced the proportion of episodes devoted to this special agenda of persuasion so that they would never overwhelm the more entertaining or personally focused topics.

Melodrama was the primary mode for these episodes, and Winfrey is a master melodramatic performer. *The Global Village Revisited* is not the only volume to name melodrama as the chief vehicle of Winfrey's offerings. Jane Shattuc in *The Talking Cure* has already made the claim. However, in her book on talk shows as well as much in her other scholarly oeuvre, Shattuc has considered melodrama and other arguably artistic modes as aesthetically degraded formulaic genres that require little close or formal attention. Yet one has to account for the differences between Winfrey's recent political melodrama and other television texts that on first glance appear to be similar. In the 2006 civic-oriented episodes of *Oprah*, Winfrey draws from the rhetoric of television journalism, as well as documentary (both the film and television varieties). Like rhetoric in classical Greece and Rome, Winfrey's effectively mines art—in this case, visual more than literary—for its potential to move its audience emotionally and to create a sense of magnitude. Much television news, especially cable news, has been issuing its reportage by way of melodrama for some time. Indeed, Winfrey has been blamed for inspiring this phenomenon. But Winfrey's shows are different, and, perhaps among their audience, more effective.

While cable television news often strikes loud notes of the scale of melodramatic excess, its foregrounding of technology and its rapid delivery by young and comely news anchors lacks the gravitas that melodramatic rhetoric relies on for its deepest expression. In the 2006 civic-oriented episodes, melodrama is either used sparingly and in relation to other kinds of rhetoric (especially true of the town hall and global warming episodes) or more profoundly, with a borrowing from serious investigative journalism or art film documentary. Just as in cable television news, celebrity and good looks are traded on (Anderson Cooper and Lisa Ling acting as *Oprah* "correspondents"), but they are used to a different end. The object is not to sell but to move the audience out of complacency and into an active support of liberal causes. The qualitative difference is considerable. The narratives are longer, like the sketches on *Slavi*, transpiring over twenty or more minutes; furthermore, within that frame, time slows down. *Oprah's* audience is predominantly mature and feminine, as opposed to the audience assumed for much of U.S. television, which is pitched at the young and the masculine. The artistry of the show assumes an audience capacity to take in longer draughts of the quotidian and to imbue them with higher meaning. The requirement of women to attend to the needs of others, sometimes seen as a fault in need of correction by certain second-wave feminists (as well as right-wing philosophers like Ayn Rand), has apparently made a different kind of television popular in the early twenty-first century, a feminine melodramatic news rhetoric. For at least two hundred years, melodrama has been inviting American women into citizenship. These new talk shows revolutionize the afternoon genre and attempt to persuade its audience into a more active role in mainstream democracy. This is a democratic vision that seeks to expand the boundaries of the nation, but rarely extends beyond those boundaries, even when the subject is a war that is prosecuted half a world away. Such is the political aesthetic of the civic-oriented *Oprah*.

Conversation Across Global Villages

What do we learn when we compare these shows to each other? In all three of these shows, genre is much more than a hostage to formula. It is, as Bakhtin would have predicted, at once a form for understanding the world and a creative response to it. The televisual genre of the talk show, even when narrowed to the civic-oriented type, is various indeed and dependent upon context—local, regional, national, target audience, historical circumstance—for its ultimate shaping. The host's and producers' own talents and proclivities enter into the creative formulation. All successful television must turn a keen eye to its audience, but these programs in particular follow the dictum of ancient rhetoric to appeal to the audience in a sensuous performance. The *Oprah Winfrey Show* borrows often from film, *Showto Na Slavi* from stage, and *Jan Publiek* from ordinary conversation, as each employs comic and melodramatic genres suitable to the task at hand. These two basic artistic genres may be planned and scripted or may arise spontaneously, so central are they to the expression of these human actors.

Conversation Across Borders

Whatever kinds of cosmopolitanism may be possible in the future, we humbly offer our three case studies as an example of both the need for crossing national boundaries and for the rewards inherent in such serious travel. Interestingly, the need may follow the rewards: we might not realize our lack until we experience the gain. One can enjoy vicariously the prospect of Simone being recognized in the streets of Antwerp; one can feel the tension between Albert and Fatiya in the "Migrant Riots" episode of *Jan Publiek*. One can thrill to the kinetic energy of *Showto Na Slavi*, and learn about Bulgarian history, Balkan regional and world politics, music, and art. Through *Oprah* one can experience something of poverty or the devastation of a hurricane, and the melodramatic representation of people suffering in a country of riches. Adjusting from one political aesthetic to the next, one gets a sense of what it might mean to be Flemish or Bulgarian or American. From the point of view of history, one can almost observe the changing fortunes of a people as these programs address key matters of public concern. Looking at these shows altogether, one can imagine how much television could help us to expand our view of life and its possibilities, how much it could truly transport us.

Neither imperialism nor late capitalism has yet foreclosed the possibilities of good television, nor has the image so far superseded the word that good television might not also be found in the genre of the civic-oriented talk show. However, one of our regrets is the loss of the audience discussion show, once practiced by *Oprah* but best exemplified in this volume by *Jan Publiek*. It is not surprising that one of the most highly rated episodes of *Jan Publiek* was the "Migrant Riots" program. However imperfect the format, this was a conversation that Flanders and Belgium needed to have—a conversation, moreover, that has perhaps never yet been had with the degree of openness available on this television program in 1997.

In her attempt to bring together an ethnographic case study of a women's Muslim piety movement in contemporary Egypt with Western feminist and poststructuralist philosophy, Saba Mahmood requires us, and herself, to consider whether our notions of democratic enlightenment ought to be visited upon others: "Do my political visions ever run up against the responsibility that I incur for the destruction of life forms so that 'unenlightened' women may be taught to live more freely?" (197–98).

> My prejudices against their forms of life (or, for that matter, theirs against mine) could not be reconciled and assimilated with "a cosmopolitan horizon" (Mehta 1999, 22); the unseemliness of differences could not be synthesized. Nor did I find myself capable of factoring this difference into my old calculus of what in their behavior had more "feminist potential" and what was hopelessly irrecuperable. (198)

Mahmood desires what we also desire, an "attempt at comprehension" across national and cultural boundaries (199). Her suggestion is to perform "analysis as a mode of conversation, rather than mastery" (199). In his book on cosmopolitanism, Kwame Anthony Appiah also puts much stock in the idea of conversation across national boundaries, a conversation that is "rich in the language of value," as are art, "[f]olktales, drama, opera, short stories" (30). We would add to this list television talk shows and other popular, mass-mediated forms.

The more technological among us often have high hopes for the Internet as a means of enabling conversation worldwide. But technology itself can be a form of mastery. Many U.S. college students, for example, find it difficult to attend to any television or film text that does not maintain not only the highest production standards but an aesthetic of fast-cutting razzle-dazzle. Some come to class with laptops and cell phones, which, while connecting them to others perhaps similar to themselves, almost physically separate them from the human diversity that may exist in their immediate surroundings. It may be as John Dewey said some years ago that democracy begins in conversation. Increasingly, it is clear that such conversation is an advanced art, the forms and methods of which depend on constant renewal.

~

Works Cited

Abbas, Tahir. *Islamic Political Radicalism: A European Perspective*. Edinburgh: Edinburgh University Press, 2007.

Adorno, Theodor, and Max Horkheimer. *Dialectic of Enlightenment*. Ed. Guenzelin Schmid Noerr. Trans. Edmund Jephcott. Stanford, CA: Stanford University Press, 2002.

Anderson, Benedict. *Imagined Communities: Reflections on the Origin and Spread of Nationalism*. London and New York: Verso, 1983.

Ang, Ien. *Watching Dallas: Soap Operas and the Melodramatic Imagination*. London: Routledge, 1985.

Anonymous. "Bulgaria: Vanishing Nation." *World Press Review* (March 2004): 28.

Appadurai, Arjun. *Modernity at Large: Cultural Dimensions of Globalization*. Minneapolis: University of Minnesota Press, 1996.

Appiah, Kwame Anthony. *Cosmopolitanism in a World of Strangers*. New York: W. W. Norton, 2006.

Arblaster, Paul. *A History of the Low Countries*. New York: Palgrave Macmillan, 2006.

Aristotle. *Poetics*. Trans. W. Rhys Roberts. Cambridge, MA: Harvard University Press, 1996.

———. *Rhetoric*. Trans. J. H. Freese. Cambridge, MA: Harvard University Press, 2006.

Austin, J. L. *How to Do Things with Words*. Cambridge, MA: Harvard University Press, 1975.

Bakhtin, M. M. "Discourse in the Novel." *The Dialogic Imagination*. Ed. Michael Holquist. Trans. Caryl Emerson and Michael Holquist. Austin: University of Texas Press, 1982.

119

———. *Rabelais and His World*. Trans. Helen Iswolsky. Bloomington: Indiana University Press, 1984.

———. *Speech Genres and Other Late Essays*. Ed. Caryl Emerson and Michael Holquist. Trans. Vern W. McGee. Austin: University of Texas Press, 1986.

Barilli, Renato. *Rhetoric*. Minneapolis: University of Minnesota Press, 1989.

Baudrillard, Jean. *Simulacra and Simulation*. Trans. Sheila Faria Glaser. Ann Arbor: University of Michigan Press, 1994.

Bennett, Tony, et al., eds. *New Keywords: A Revised Vocabulary of Culture and Society*. Oxford: Blackwell Publishing, 2005.

Bennett, W. Lance. *News: The Politics of Illusion*. New York: Longman, 1988.

Berube, Michael, ed. *The Aesthetics of Cultural Studies*. Oxford: Blackwell, 2005.

Bhabha, Homi, ed. *Nation and Narration*. London and New York: Routledge, 1990.

———. "Introduction: Narrating the Nation." In Bhabha, *Nation And Narration*, 1–7.

———. "DissemiNation: Time, Narrative, and the Margins of the Modern Nation." In Bhabha, *Nation and Narration*, 291–322.

Bolter, Jay David, and Richard Grusin. *Remediation: Understanding New Media*. Cambridge, MA: MIT Press, 2000.

Booth, William. "One Nation, Indivisible: Is It History?" *The Washington Post* (online), 22 February 1998 (A1), www.washingtonpost.com/wp-srv/national/longterm/meltingpot/melt0222.htm.

Bremmer, Jan. "Mythology." *The Oxford Classical Dictionary*. Ed. Simon Hornblower and Antony Spawforth. Oxford: Oxford University Press, 2003.

Brinkley, Douglas. *The Great Deluge: Hurricane Katrina, New Orleans, and the Mississippi Gulf Coast*. New York: HarperCollins, 2007.

Brooks, Peter. *The Melodramatic Imagination: Balzac, Henry James, Melodrama and The Mode of Excess*. New Haven, CT: Yale University Press, 1995.

Brunvatne, Raina, and Andrew Tolson. "'It Makes It OK To Cry': Two Types of 'Therapy Talk' in TV Talk Shows." In Tolson, *Television Talk Shows*, 139–54.

Bourdieu, Pierre. *Distinction: A Social Critique of the Judgement of Taste*. Trans. Richard Nice. Cambridge, MA: Harvard University Press, 1984.

Butler, Judith. *Bodies that Matter: On the Discursive Limits of Sex*. New York: Routledge, 1993.

Carpentier, Nico. "Managing Audience Participation." *European Journal of Communication* 16, no. 2 (2001): 209–32.

Cazden, Courtney. *Classroom Discourse: The Language of Teaching and Learning*. Portsmouth, NH: Heinemann, 1988.

Chalaby, Jean K., ed. *Transnational Television Worldwide: Towards a New Media Order*. London and New York: I. B. Taurus, 2005.

———. "Towards an Understanding of Media Transnationalism." In Chalaby, *Transnational Television Worldwide*, 1–13.

———. "The Quiet Invention of a New Medium: Twenty Years of Trans-National Television in Europe." In Chalaby, *Transnational Television Worldwide*, 43–65.

Cicero. *On Oratory and Orators*. Trans. J. S. Watson. Carbondale: Southern Illinois University Press, 1986.

Clark, Katerina, and Michael Holquist. *Mikhail Bakhtin*. Cambridge, MA: Belknap Press, 1984.

Corner, John. *Studying Media: Problems of Theory and Method*. Edinburgh: Edinburgh University Press, 1998.

Crampton, R. J. *Aleksandur Stamboliiski: Bulgaria*. London: Haus Histories, 2009.

———. *A Concise History of Bulgaria*. Cambridge: Cambridge University Press, 1997.

Curtin, Michael. "Media Capitals: Cultural Geographies of Global TV." In Spigel and Olsson, *Television After TV*, 270–302.

Davis, Kimberly Chabot. "Oprah's Book Club and the Politics of Cross Racial Empathy." *International Journal of Cultural Studies* 7, no. 4 (2004): 399–419.

Dewey, John. *Dialogue with John Dewey*. Ed. Corliss Lamont. New York: Horizon Press, 1959.

D'Haenens, Leen, and Frieda Saeys, eds. *Western Broadcasting at the Dawn of the 21st Century*. Berlin: Mouton de Gruyter, 2001.

Dhoest, Alexander. "Quality As/And National Identity: Press Discourse on Flemish Period TV Drama." *European Journal of Cultural Studies* 7, no. 3 (2004): 305–24.

———. "Reconstructing Flanders: The Representation of the Nation In Flemish Period Drama." *Communications* 28 (2003): 253–74.

Dilov, Lyuben, Jr. Interview. Sofia: 9 June 2003.

Dimitrov, Vesselin. *Bulgaria: The Uneven Transition*. London: Routledge, 2001.

Dewinter, Filip. "Belgium, Eurabization Report 2007." www.filipdewinter.be.

Dixon, Kathleen. "The Dialogic Genres of Oprah Winfrey's 'Crying Shame.'" *Journal of Popular Culture* 35, no. 2 (Fall 2001): 171–91.

Dixon, Kathleen, and Daniela Koleva. "Affirming and Challenging Baudrillard, Or Some Women of the Global Village." *International Journal of Baudrillard Studies* 4, no. 2 (March 2007), www.ubishops.ca/BaudrillardStudies/vol4_2/v4-2-dixon-koleva.html.

Dixon, Kathleen, and Sonja Spee. "Deploying Identity for Democratic Ends." *The European Journal of Women's Studies* 10, no. 4 (November 2003): 409–22.

Eco, Umberto. *Travels in Hyperreality*. New York: Harcourt Brace, 1986.

Elsaesser, Thomas. "Tales of Sound and Fury: Observations on the Family Melodrama." In Gledhill, *Home is Where the Heart Is*, 43–69.

Fanon, Frantz. *The Wretched of the Earth*. New York: Weidenfeld, 1963.

Farr, Cecilia Konchar. *Reading Oprah: How Oprah's Book Club Changed America*. Albany: State University of New York Press, 2004.

Fiske, John. *Television Culture*. London: Routledge, 1987.

Flaccus, Quintus Horacius. *Horace, II. Satires, Epistles, The Art of Poetry*. Trans. H. Rushton Fairclough. Cambridge, MA: Harvard University Press (Loeb Classical Library), 1926.

Fraser, Nancy. "Politics, Culture and the Public Sphere: Toward a Postmodern Conception." In Nicholson and Seidman, *Social Postmodernism*, 287–314.

Frye, Northrup. *Anatomy of Criticism*. Princeton, NJ: Princeton University Press, 1957.

Gamson, Joshua. *Freaks Talk Back: Tabloid Talk Shows and Sexual Nonconformity*. Chicago: University of Chicago Press, 1998.

Genosko, Gary. *McLuhan and Baudrillard: Masters*. New York: Routledge, 2002.

Geraghty, Christine. "Discussing Quality: Critical Vocabularies and Popular Television Drama." *Media and Cultural Theory*. Ed. James Curran and David Morley. London: Routledge, 2006.

Gerrie, James. "Canada's Lost Tradition of Technological Criticism." *The River of History: Trans-National and Trans-Disciplinary Perspectives on the Immanence of the Past*. Calgary: University of Calgary Press, 2005.

Graves, Robert. *The Greek Myths*. London: The Folio Society, 1996.

Grindstaff, Laura. *The Money Shot: Trash, Class, and the Making of TV Talk Show*. Chicago: University of Chicago Press, 2002.

Gledhill, Christine, ed. *Home is Where the Heart Is: Studies in Melodrama and the Woman's Film*. London: British Film Institute, 1987.

Greenwald, Robert, and Alexandra Kitty. *Outfoxed* (DVD). New York: The Disinformation Company, 2005.

Haag, Laurie. "Oprah Winfrey: The Construction of Intimacy in the Talk Show Setting." *Journal of Popular Culture* 26, no. 4 (Spring 1993): 115–21.

Haarman, Louann. "Performing Talk." In Tolson, *Television Talk Shows*, 31–64.

Hall, R. Mark. "The 'Oprahfication' of Literacy: Reading 'Oprah's Book Club.'" *College English* 65, no. 6 (July 2003): 646–67.

Harnish, Robert M. "Communicating with Proverbs." *Communication and Cognition* 26, nos. 3–4 (1993): 265–89.

Illouz, Eva. *Oprah Winfrey and the Glamour of Misery: An Essay on Popular Culture*. New York: Columbia University Press, 2003.

———. *Saving the Modern Soul: Therapy, Emotions, and the Culture of Self-Help*. Berkeley: University of California Press, 2008.

Jacobs, Jason. "Issues of Judgment and Value in Television Studies." *International Journal of Cultural Studies* 4, no. 4 (2001): 427–47.

Jenkins, Henry. *Convergence Culture: Where Old and New Media Collide*. Albany: New York University Press, 2008.

Judt, Tony. *Postwar: A History of Europe Since 1945*. London: Penguin Press, 2005.

Keeter, Scott, et al. *Favorability of Leading Figures: Opinion of Oprah More Politicized*. Washington, DC: PEW Research Center: 14 May 2008. News release. people-press.org/reports/pdf/422.pdf.

Koehn, Nancy, and Erica Helms. *Oprah Winfrey*. Cambridge, MA: Harvard Business School Publishing, 2003.

Lapham, Lewis. "Introduction to the MIT Press Edition." In McLuhan, *Understanding Media*, ix–xxiii.

Lee, Paul S. N. "Television and Global Culture: Assessing the Role of Television In Globalization." In Wang and Servaes, *The New Communications Landscape*, 188–98.

Livingstone, Sonia, and Peter Lunt. *Talk on Television: Audience Participation and Public Debate*. London: Routledge, 1993.

Madden, David. *Harlequin's Stick, Charlie's Cane: A Comparative Study of Commedia Dell'arte and Silent Stapstick Comedy*. Bowling Green, KY: Popular Press, 1975.

MacLeish, Kenneth. "Editor's Introduction." In Graves, *The Greek Myths*, 11–20.

Mahmood, Saba. *The Politics of Piety: The Islamic Revival and the Feminist Subject*. Princeton, NJ, and Oxford: Princeton University Press, 2005.

Manga, Julie. *Talking Trash: The Cultural Politics of Daytime TV Talk Shows*. New York and London: New York University Press, 2003.

Marchand, Philip. *Marshall McLuhan: The Medium and The Messenger*. Cambridge, MA: MIT Press, 1989.

Masciarotte, Gloria-Jean. "C'mon Girl: Oprah Winfrey and the Discourse of Feminine Talk." *Genders* 11 (1991): 81–110.

McLuhan, Marshall. *The Gutenberg Galaxy: The Making of Typographic Man*. Toronto: University of Toronto Press, 1962.

———. *Understanding Media: The Extensions of Man*. Cambridge, MA: MIT Press, 1994.

MediaLinks. "Slavi Show Audience: January–May 2003." Sofia, Bulgaria.

Michielsens, Magda. *Vrouwen in de Kijker. Hoe Brengen TV1 en TV2 de Vrouw in Beeld?* Brussels: BRTN, 1991.

Miller, Susan. *Textual Carnivals: The Politics of Composition*. Carbondale: Southern Illinois University Press, 1991.

Mitchell, W. J. T. "Aesthetics." In Bennett et al., *New Keywords*, 1–3.

Mittell, Jason. *Genre and Television: From Cop Shows to Cartoons in American Culture*. New York: Routledge, 2004.

Moseley, Rachel. "Makeover Takeover on British Television." *Screen* 41, no. 3 (Autumn 2000): 299–314.

Mukhopandhyay, Alok Rashmi. "Radical Islam in Europe: Misperceptions and Misconceptions." In Abbas, *Islamic Political Radicalism*, 99–116.

Munson, Wayne. *All Talk: The Talk Show in Media Culture*. Philadelphia: Temple University Press, 1994.

National Public Radio. "Obama Election Prompts Soul-Searching." 9 January 2009. www.npr.org/templates/story/story.php?storyId=99189120.

Neale, Steve, and Frank Krutnik. *Popular Film and Television Comedy*. London: Routledge, 1990.

Nicholson, Linda, and Steven Seidman, eds. *Social Postmodernism: Beyond Identity Politics*. Cambridge: Cambridge University Press, 1996.

Novitz, David. "Aesthetics of Popular Art." *The Oxford Handbook of Aesthetics*. Ed. Jerrold Levinson. Oxford: Oxford University Press, 2003: 733–47.

Ogbu, John. "Immigrant and Involuntary Minorities in Perspective." *Minority Status and Schooling: A Comparative Study of Immigrant and Involuntary Minorities*. Eds. M. A. Gibson and J. U. Ogbu. New York: Garland.

Ong, Walter. *Orality and Literacy*. New York: Routledge, 2002 (1982).

Paglia, Camille. "Introduction." *Break, Blow, Burn*. New York: Pantheon, 2005: vii–xvii.

Parenti, Michael. *The Assasination of Julius Caesar: A People's History of Ancient Rome*. New York: New Press, 2004.

Peck, Janice. *The Age of Oprah: Cultural Icon for the Neoliberal Era*. Boulder, CO: Paradigm Publishers, 2008.

———. "Talk About Race: Framing a Popular Discourse of Race on Oprah Winfrey." *Cultural Critique* 27 (Spring 1994): 89–126.

Peckham, Robert Shannon. *Rethinking Heritage: Cultures and Politics in Europe*. London: I. B. Taurus, 2003.

Pollack, Sheldon, et al., eds. *Cosmopolitanism*. Durham, NC: Duke University Press, 2002.

Propp, Vladimir. *Morphology of the Folktale*. Ed. Louis Wagner. Trans. Laurence Scott. Austin: University of Texas Press, 1968.

Radin, Paul. *The Trickster: A Study in American Indian Mythology*. New York: Schocken Books, 1972.

Radway, Janice. *Reading the Romance: Women, Patriarchy and Popular Literature*. Chapel Hill: University of North Carolina Press, 1984.

Rapping, Elayne. *The Culture of Recovery*. Boston: Beacon Press, 1997.

Rooney, Kathleen. *Reading with Oprah: The Book Club that Changed America*. Fayetteville: University of Arkansas Press, 2005.

Rose, Brian. "The Talk Show." *TV Genres*. Ed. Brian Rose. Westport, CT: Greenwood Press, 1985.

Santo, Avi. "Nunavut: Inuit Television and Cultural Citizenship." *International Journal of Cultural Studies* 7, no. 4 (2004): 379–97.

Shattuc, Jane M. "The Shifting Terrain of American Talk Shows." In Wasko, *A Companion To Television*, 324–36.

———. *The Talking Cure: TV Talk Shows and Women*. New York: Routledge, 1997.

———. "Television Production: Who Makes American TV?" In Wasko, *A Companion To Television*, 142–56.

Shumway, David. "Cultural Studies and Questions of Pleasure and Value." In Berube, *The Aesthetics of Cultural Studies*, 103–16.

Sinclair, John. "International Television Channels in the Latin American Audio-Visual Space." In Chalaby, *Transnational Television Worldwide*, 196–215.

Singer, Ben. *Melodrama and Modernity*. New York: Columbia University Press, 2001.

Squire, Corrine. "Empowering Women? The Oprah Winfrey Show." *Feminism And Psychology* 4, no. 1 (1994): 63–79.

Sparks, Colin. "The Global, The Local, and the Public Sphere." In Wang and Servaes, *The New Communications Landscape*, 74–95.

Spigel, Lynn, and Jan Olsson, eds. *Television After TV: Essays on A Medium in Transition*. Durham, NC: Duke University Press, 2004.

Sterne, Jonathan. "The Burden of Culture." In Berube, *The Aesthetics of Cultural Studies*, 80–102.

Straubhaar, Joseph. "Culture, Language, and Social Class in the Globalization of Television." In Wang and Servaes, *The New Communications Landscape*, 199–224.

Straubhaar, Joseph, and Luiz G. Duarte. "Adapting US Transnational Television Channels to a Complex World: From Cultural Imperialism to Localization To Hybridization." In Chalaby, *Transnational Television Worldwide*, 216–53.

Striphas, Ted. "A Dialectic with the Everyday: Communication and Cultural Politics On Oprah Winfrey's Book Club." *Critical Studies in Media Communications* 20, no. 3 (September 2003): 295–317.

Tibi, Bassam. *Political Islam, World Politics, and Europe: Democratic Peace and Euro-Islam versus Global Jihad*. London: Routledge, 2008.

Timberg, Bernard M. *Television Talk: A History of the TV Talk Show*. Austin: University of Texas Press, 2002.

Tolson, Andrew, ed. *Television Talk Shows: Discourse, Performance, Spectacle*. Mahwah, NJ: Lawrence Erlbaum Associates, Inc., 2001.

Tyrrell, Ian. "American Exceptionalism in an Age of International History." *The American Historical Review* 96, no. 4 (1991): 1031–55.

Van Rompaey, Jan. Interview. Antwerp: December 1998.

Vazov, Ivan. *Under the Yoke: A Romance of Bulgarian Liberty*. Boston: Adamant Media Corporation, 2007 (1893).

VRT. "Beheersovereenkomst 1997–2001." Brussels: VRT, 1997.

Wang, Georgette, and Jan Servaes. *The New Communications Landscape: Demystifying Media Globalization*. London: Routledge, 2000.

Wasko, Janet, ed. *A Companion To Television*. Oxford: Blackwell Publishing, 2005.

Waterfield, Bruno. "Don't Confuse Terrorism with Islam, says EU." *Telegraph.Co.uk*. 31 March 2007. www.telegraph.co.uk/news/worldnews/1547133/Dont-confuse-terrorism-with-Islam-says-EU.html.

Williams, Linda. *Playing the Race Card: Melodramas in Black and White*. Princeton, NJ: Princeton University Press, 2001.

Wilson, Tony. "Playfully Becoming the 'Other': Watching *Oprah Winfrey* On Malaysian Television." *International Journal of Cultural Studies* 4, no. 1 (2001): 88–110.

Wood, Helen. "'No, YOU Rioted!' The Pursuit of Conflict in the Management of 'Lay' and 'Expert' Discourses on *Kilroy*." In Tolson, *Television Talk Shows*, 65–88.

Wolff, Janet. "Groundless Beauty: Feminism and the Aesthetics of Uncertainty." *Feminist Theory* 7, no. 2 (2006): 143–58.

Young, Iris Marion. *Inclusion and Democracy*. Oxford: Oxford University Press, 2002.

Index

age, 10, 42, 47–50
aesthetics, 50–53, 120, 123, 124, 125;
    Bourdieu and, 17, 50; cultural studies
    and, 17–18, 84; *East Enders*, 17; *Jan
    Publiek*, 34–36, 39, 41, 46, 49–50;
    Kant and, 22; melodramatic, 53,
    91–94; *Oprah Winfrey Show*, 87,
    91–94; popular, 17–18; rhetoric
    and, 36; *Showto Na Slavi*, 70–72, 84;
    value and, 17. *See also* art; comedy;
    melodrama; political aesthetic
Angel Network, 100, 107
Antwerp. *See* Flanders
Appadurai, Arjun, 1, 9, 10, 119
art, 2, 3–4, 5–6, 8, 17, 19, 20, 22,
    25–26; Adorno and, 18; Bakhtin
    and, 23; contemporary, 22; cultural
    studies and, 16–17; entertainment
    and, 6, 22; excellence and, 5;
    feminism and, 17; folk culture and
    18; genre and, 25; McLuhan's view
    of, 7–8, 18; oral cultures and, 18;
    poetics and, 18; politics and 3, 5, 17,
    23; popular, 3, 11, 17–19, 21, 23;
    popular, democratic potential of, 17;

rhetoric and, 2, 4, 19–23, 24; *Showto
    Na Slavi* and, 5; television and, 8,
    17–18, 25–26; television talk shows
    and, 4, 5, 16, 23; visual, 18. *See also*
    aesthetics; comedy; melodrama
audience, 1, 3, 4, 10, 16–17, 19, 23, 24,
    25, 26, 116; democracy and, 94; *Jan
    Publiek*, 5, 29, 32, 34–35, 38–39, 40,
    42, 43, 46, 49, 50, 51, 52, 55, 84, 112,
    113; niche, 6, 111; *Oprah Winfrey
    Show*, 6, 85, 86, 87, 89–90, 92, 93,
    94, 95, 98–100, 101, 102, 103, 104–5,
    114–15, 116; share (or ratings), 6, 34,
    65, 112; *Showto Na Slavi*, 5, 70–71,
    72, 73, 75, 76–77, 79, 80, 81, 83, 84,
    110; studio, 4, 16, 31, 34, 38, 70, 77,
    81, 90, 93, 98, 100; surveys, 36. *See
    also* MediaLinks; rhetoric
audience discussion shows. *See*
    television talk shows
Austin, J. L., 24–25, 41, 82

Balkan News Corp, 6, 65
Balkan(s): Belgium and, 112; Bulgaria
    and, 109, 112, 117; Mountains, 71,

127

74, 78; people, 112; region, 117; Wars, 109

Bakhtin, M. M.: carnival and, 9, 20, 21; centrifugal and centripetal forces, 111; the comic and, 21; democratic discourse, 24; dialogic, 24, 56, 83, 84, 101; dialogism, 24, 51; epideictic rhetoric and, 20; ideologeme, 24; internally persuasive, 56, 74; monologic, 24, 56; official discourse, 24; parody, 74; reaccentuation, 74; speech genres, 23, 24, 25, 67, 116; stratification, 24; utterance, 23, 24, 25

Barilli, Renato, 2, 19–20, 22, 23, 24

Belgium: Brussels, capital city of, 5, 27, 29, 31, 56; Catholics in, 27; Europeanness, 27; federalization of, 28; geography of, 27; history of, 27; homosexuality and Islam in, 57; immigrants of, 29, 38, 53, 54–61; Islam in, 54–55, 57–61; king of, 35; language of, 27, 28; television, 28–29, 30, 31; violence in, 54; Walloonia, 27, 28, 56; welfare state, 27, 28–29. See also Flanders; Jan Publiek; Van Rompaey, Jan; VRT

Bhabha, Homi, 11, 14, 15

Bourdieu, Pierre, 17, 22, 50

BTV (Bulgarian television network), 26, 65, 70, 76

Bulgaria, 2, 5; agrarian past of, 63, 68, 111, 112; "Belgium of the Balkans," 112; brigadier movement of, 76, 78; capitalism in, 63–64, 72; capital city of (Sofia), 68; chalga music of, 63, 68; citizen of, 110; Communist era of, 16, 69, 74, 76; corruption in, 63–64, 68; cultural studies of, 67; culture of, 16, 64, 69, 70–72, 83; declining birthrate of, 64; democracy in, 77; diaspora of, 112; East-West divide in, 63–64, 73; emigration from, 64, 80–81; England, relations with, 110;

European Union, member of, 10, 64; Germany, relations with, 110; globalization of, 72, 112, 117; history of, 10, 63–64, 68–69, 72, 74–75, 83, 117; hush (nineteenth-century revolutionary), 68; identity, national, of, 78, 83, 109, 117; intellectuals of, 110, 112; kritchma (village tavern), 26, 70; language of, 65, 72, 76, 80, 81, 84; minorities, treatment of, 109; modernization of, 74; mutra, 68; nationalism of, 16, 68; National Revival Period, 83; Orthodox Christianity of, 70; Ottoman Empire, subject to, 63; peasants, 74–75, 111, 112; people of, 5, 6, 10, 26, 64–65, 77, 79–84; politics of, 73, 110; popular aesthetic of, 70–72; popular culture of, 110; poverty of, 10, 64, 68; Russia, relations with, 83, 110; Serbia, attitudes toward, 70; Simeon, Boris (prime minister, former tsar), 68, 78; Slavic countries, identification with, 70, 112; Stamboliiski, Alexander (prime minister), 112; Stoilov, Konstantin (prime minister), 112; television of, 72; Turkey, relations to, 63; "Videnov's Winter," 64–65; "wealth" of, 111. See also audience; Balkan News Corp; Balkan(s); BTV; Showto Na Slavi

Bush, George W., 85, 86, 94, 96, 97, 98–99, 115

carnival. See Bakhtin, M. M.

capitalism, 11, 18, 71, 72, 91, 92, 96, 117

Carpentier, Nico, 4, 16, 33, 36, 61, 84

celebrity, 5, 6, 34, 40, 41, 47, 48, 52, 53, 69, 70, 88–89, 101, 102, 110, 116

citizen, 5, 6, 13, 16, 23, 29, 31, 33, 43, 44, 47, 50, 55, 62, 66, 85, 94, 98, 100, 107, 109, 110, 114, 116

class, 3, 4, 6, 8, 9, 10, 14, 20, 21, 22, 24, 32, 33, 39, 43, 46, 48, 49, 50, 51, 52, 54, 57, 58, 87–92, 94, 95, 96, 106, 112, 113, 114, 115. *See also* aesthetics; Bourdieu, Pierre; cultural studies
comedy, 3, 15, 20–21, 22, 64, 76; commedia dell-arte, 67; democratic nature of, 21; jokes, 8, 21, 25, 39, 43–45, 48, 49, 69, 70, 75, 79, 80, 83, 89, 110; Karagoz, Karagiosi, 67; melodrama, relation to, 22; myth and, 67; "nonnarrative" (skits, sketches, gags, jokes), 21; Punch and Judy, 67; sketches, 21, 22, 69, 70, 116; spectacle and, 22, 24; variety show and, 114. *See also* narrative; satire
cosmopolitanism, 109, 117, 118
Crampton, R. J., 109, 112
Cuckoo Band. *See Showto Na Slavi*
cultural studies, 1, 2, 3, 6, 10, 16–19, 22, 67, 72, 84. *See also* aesthetics; Belgium; Bulgaria; class; Flanders; United States

democracy, 4, 13, 19, 41, 53, 65, 77, 91, 116, 118; Bulgaria and, 112; carnival and, 111; Fiske's "semiotic democracy," 74. *See also Jan Publiek; Oprah Winfrey Show; Showto Na Slavi*
democratic discourse, 2, 4, 9, 24, 69, 78
Dhoest, Alexander, 11, 14–15, 114
dialogism. *See* Bakhtin, M. M.

egalitarian, 19, 33, 36, 37, 51, 55, 112–13
ethics, 17, 37, 107; democratic, 24
ethos. *See* rhetoric

Fanon, Frantz, 14, 15, 121; national culture, 16
feminist, 4, 17, 32, 39, 86, 88, 89, 90, 111, 116, 117, 118

Flanders, 27; Antwerp, capital city of, 5, 29, 38, 47, 54, 117; "cultural emancipation" of, 15; culture of, 14, 15, 28, 29; history, 27–28; independence movement of (Vlaams Blok/Vlaams Belang), 28; language, 28–29; nationalism of, 14, 15, 114; people, 15, 28, 29; politics of, 28; population of, 27; wealth of, 27. *See also* Belgium; *Jan Publiek*; Van Rompaey, Jan; VRT

gay (homosexual), 33, 40, 45, 52, 57, 111
gender, 32, 39, 43, 49, 89, 96, 100, 113
Gellner, Ernest, 11, 12, 16, 111
global village, 7–11, 42, 109, 111. *See also* public sphere, global
Godji (Slavi sidekick). *See Showto Na Slavi*
Grindstaff, Laura, 4, 16, 70
Gutenberg Galaxy, 7, 123

Habermas, Jurgen, 9, 33, 50
Harpo Productions, 96, 107
Helms, Erica, 87, 88, 107

image, 8, 10, 14, 47, 61, 76, 88, 94, 95, 96–97, 98, 100, 105, 106, 113, 117
imagined communities, 12
imperialism, 6, 109, 110, 117
internationalism, 11, 27, 70, 72, 112. *See also* global village; public sphere

Jan Publiek: aesthetic, 34–36, 39, 41; artistry of, 18, 33–35, 38–39, 43, 47; audience of, 34, 35; camerawork on, 35–36, 42; class in, 20, 21, 32, 43–44, 46, 51; comedy in, 21, 22, 39; creation of, 18, 30–34, 37; egalitarian nature of, 15, 31–33, 36; Flemish identity of, 5, 15, 31, 33, 34, 35; gender in, 32, 37, 39, 43, 45,

47; genre of, 37; host of (see Van Rompaey, Jan); hours broadcast, 34; intimacy of, 35; Islam, discussion of, 55, 57–61; melodrama in, 22, 55; "Migrant Riots" episode, of, 53–61; music, theme, for, 35; Muslims, 54–55, 57–61, 114; nationalism in, 114; opening of, 35–36; panelist Albert, 56, 59–61, 117; panelist Betty, 37–40, 43, 47, 50, 51, 52, 56–57, 58, 113; panelist Damien, 37, 41, 42–47, 49, 51, 52, 113; panelist Fatiya, 55, 56, 59–61, 117; panelist Rudi, 37, 40–42, 44, 45, 47, 48, 49, 50, 52, 53, 57–59, 60, 113, 114; panelist Simone, 37, 42, 47–50, 52, 113, 117; political aesthetic of, 5, 20, 34, 36, 39–40, 46, 47, 49–50, 51–52, 53; politics on, 39; popularity of, 10; producers of, 36, 39, 43; public obligations of, 30; satire in, 37, 41, 42, 45, 46; set of, 34–35; speech acts and genres of, 21, 25, 37, 38–39, 40, 42, 44, 45, 48; topics on, 37, 41–42, 43–44; turn-taking on, 33, 34, 36; years broadcast, 5, 29, 30. See also audience; audience discussion shows; public sphere; Van Rompaey, Jan
Jerry Springer Show. See television talk shows
jokes. See comedy

Kilroy. See television talk shows
Koehn, Nancy, 87, 88, 107
kritchma (Bulgarian village tavern). See Bulgaria

logos. See rhetoric

mass media, 4, 42, 52, 53, 70, 113, 115; hypermediated, 7
McLuhan, Marshall, 2, 7–9, 17, 18, 20, 40, 42, 43, 109

MediaLinks, 26, 65
melodrama, 3, 6, 8, 17, 20, 21–22, 23, 25, 40, 53–54, 62, 70, 80, 86, 87, 91, 100, 101, 103–8; aesthetics of, 91–94; Islam and, 54, 55–56, 57, 58, 60, 114; mode of, 95; news, 116; rhetoric and, 95–100, 108. See also narrative; rhetoric
modernity, 12, 16, 20, 40, 42, 52, 68, 74, 84, 90, 91, 92, 94, 100, 101, 102, 103, 111; melodrama and, 20, 21, 53–54, 92, 95–96; rhetoric and, 95–96
monologic, 24, 56
Muslim, 29, 117. See also Jan Publiek; melodrama
mutra ("ugly face," mobster bodyguard). See Bulgaria
myth, 26, 46, 67–68, 80, 81, 84; definition of, 66; fans in creation of, 65–66; melting pot, 13, 54; multiculturalism, 13; trickster, 5, 21, 67, 72, 73, 76, 111

narrative, 116; comic, 21; Jan Publiek panelists in, 31, 37; melodramatic, 25, 53, 56, 91–94, 101, 106; myth and, 66; nationalist, 11, 14–15
nationalism, 11–16, 54–55, 109, 117; "American exceptionalism," 14; Anderson's definition of, 12; Bulgarian, 12, 16, 74, 83, 109–12; "cultural nationalism," 114; development of, 12; Fanon's view of, 14, 15; Flemish, 14–15, 55, 114; Gellner's definition of, 11; U.S., 12–14, 95, 98, 116
Netherlands (Holland), 10, 28, 66, 112. See also television talk shows, Het Lagerhuis
news, 48, 97, 101; "hard" news, 53, 97–98, 105–6; hybridization of, 105; media, news, 97; VRT policies

regarding, 30. *See also* melodrama; rhetoric

News Corp, 6, 65. *See also* Balkan News Corp

newspapers, 32, 48, 71, 75, 78

niche programming. *See* television

Ong, Walter, 2, 7, 20, 43, 47

O Magazine, 103

Oprah Book Club, 86, 88

Oprah.com, 103, 107

Oprah Winfrey Show: aesthetics of, 85, 86, 87, 89, 90, 92, 96, 97, 106, 117; audience, attention to, 6, 10, 85, 86, 88–90, 93, 94, 100, 101–3, 104; audience discussion show, as, 117; civic-oriented episodes of, 85–86, 92, 96–99, 101–7; class, in, 87, 88, 89, 90, 92, 94, 100, 104, 114; gender on, 85, 88, 89, 90, 94, 102, 103, 105, 106, 114; "family" on, 100, 102; fantasy episodes of, 88–90; high production quality of, 97; melodrama on, 91–94, 96, 97, 100–101, 107; news and, 95, 101, 102, 104–6, 115–16; political aesthetic of, 85, 90, 106, 110; politics of, 85, 90, 96, 101, 102, 103, 104, 106, 107; race and, 88, 90, 101, 104, 105, 106; rhetoric of, 86, 85, 91, 95, 107–8, 116; variety on, 101. *See also* audience; rhetoric

orality, 7, 42, 43; secondary orality, 47

participation: democratic, 6, 111, 112; McLuhan and, 7–9, 18, 20, 42

pathos. *See* rhetoric

peasant, 74–75, 111, 112

performance, 1, 3, 5, 9, 16, 19, 21, 23, 26, 42, 43, 50–53, 69, 73–79, 80, 83, 87, 96, 117

performative, 25, 47, 83

poetics, 18, 19, 20, 91; popular, 2; rhetoric and, 2, 19

political aesthetic, 2, 16, 20, 40, 42, 47, 50, 55, 62, 110–11, 112–13, 114, 116, 117. *See also Jan Publiek*; *Oprah Winfrey Show*; *Showto Na Slavi*

politics: democratic, 3, 4, 36, 111; institutions, 29, 53; popular, 3. *See also Jan Publiek*; *Oprah Winfrey Show*; *Showto Na Slavi*

popular art, 2, 3, 11, 67, 90, 91, 97; rhetoric and, 23

popular culture, 66, 69, 86, 95, 110, 112, 118; scholarship on, 2

public sphere, 4, 9; democratic, 50; diasporic, 10; gender in, 29, 39, 100; global, 5, 10; inequality and, 50; *Jan Publiek* and, 50; *Oprah Winfrey Show* and, 86; rhetoric in, 95, 100; *Showto Na Slavi* and, 84

race, 12, 13, 43, 87, 88, 90, 101, 104, 105, 106

religion, 29, 53, 66; Catholic, 27; Islam, 46, 54–61, 114, 117; Orthodox Christianity, 70; Protestant, 27

rhetoric, 18, 75, 107–8; action and, 98, 101; aesthetic and, 38–40, 87; African American, 87; Aristotle's theory of, 19, 95; art of, 24, 36, 84, 88, 90, 95; audience and, 19, 24, 85; Cicero and orators, 19; classical, 1–2, 3, 19–20, 22, 116; commercial, 40, 42, 113; democratic, 4, 11, 19, 98; delivery of, 96; didactic, 38; electronic, 96; eloquence, 19; epideictic, 20; ethos, 19, 23, 24, 38, 40, 50, 53, 74, 88, 94, 95, 101, 102, 104, 105, 107; gender and, 38, 39, 95, 101, 102; images and, 96; logos, 20, 23, 53, 55, 95, 101; melodrama and, 22, 86, 91, 93, 94, 95–100, 101, 106, 107, 116; New Age, 87; news, 101, 106, 116; pathos, 53, 95, 96, 101, 105, 114; performance of,

1, 46–47, 51–52, 96; Plato's view of, 95; political, 3, 84, 86; political aesthetic, 2, 86, 113; talent in, 46, 47, 57, 96, 97–98, 101–2, 115; television and, 22, 85, 115. *See also* poetics; popular art; speech genre

satire, 37, 41, 42, 45, 46, 110; political, 5, 64, 68, 73, 76–77, 79, 110. *See also Jan Publiek; Oprah Winfrey Show; Showto Na Slavi;* Van Rompaey, Jan
sexuality, 44, 45, 49, 57, 67, 68, 71, 76, 89–90, 111
Shattuc, Jane, 3, 4, 5, 25–26, 86, 94, 115
Showto Na Slavi: aesthetic, 70–72, 74, 111; benediction on, 83; Bulgarian identity on, 64–65, 68, 71–72, 77–78, 81, 83, 109–10; cocreator of (Lyuben Dilov Jr.), 64, 65, 68, 69, 111, 112; Communism satirized on, 74–75, 76–77, 78–79; Cuckoo Band, 65, 68; democracy on, 110; ensemble of, 78–79; excess of, 69, 71, 74; folktale speech genre, 80; Godji (Slavi sidekick) on, 69, 71, 73–76, 77, 78–79; guests on, 70, 80, 84; history represented on, 64, 68, 72, 83, 84; internationalism on, 70, 112; music on, 63, 68, 70–71, 75, 76, 82, 83; myth on, 67–68; nationalism in, 16, 64, 109–12; political aesthetic, 111; politics and, 73, 110; popular aesthetic, 70–72; popularity of, 65; production values of, 72; proverbs on, 83–84; ritual, 72, 80; satire on, 5, 64, 68, 73, 74, 76–77, 79, 110; Slavic countries represented on, 70, 112; stage, the, 69; theme song of, 72, 76; translators on, 70; vox populi, CD of, 65
Slavi Show. See Showto Na Slavi
speech act, 24, 41, 42, 44, 47, 52, 74, 89

speech genre, 23, 24–26, 36–50, 51, 57, 58, 59, 72, 73, 74, 77, 80–81, 83, 88, 89, 98, 103, 105, 110, 112, 113, 114

television: audience of, 116; cable and satellite, 6; commercial, 6, 29–30, 112, 113; cross-cultural potential of, 117–18; democratic fare, 6; foreign programming on, 5, 6, 9; Fox News Network, 86; gender on, 94; "good," 1, 2, 117; hypermediated, 7, 88, 90; industrial production of, 3; media imperialism of, 9, 112; melodrama on, 94, 95; news on, 85, 88, 95, 96, 97, 102, 103, 105, 115–16; niche programming of, 6, 10, 66, 111; ownership of, 6, 9, 65, 96, 105, 107; participation in (McLuhan's concept), 7–9, 18; public, 9, 18, 29–30; ritual on, 72; stage, borrows from, 69, 90; studies on, 2, 4, 6; U.S., 116. *See also* global village; McLuhan, Marshall; television talk shows
television talk shows, 2, 6; afternoon, 3, 5, 6, 31, 37, 39, 45, 48, 70, 80, 85, 87–88, 94, 98, 100, 116; artful, 4, 5, 16, 23; audience discussion shows, 3, 4, 5, 31, 33–34, 37, 47, 50, 56, 62, 69, 112, 117; civic-oriented, 3–4; democratic aims of, 4, 5, 6, 31, 88, 89, 114, 116; *Het Lagerhuis* (The Lower House), 5, 31, 33, 37; hosts of, 4, 5, 6, 21, 30–32, 34, 35, 37, 39, 43, 44–47, 48–49, 50, 51, 52, 55, 61, 67, 69, 71, 78, 90, 94, 98, 102, 106, 112–13, 115; hybridity, 3; *Kilroy,* 5, 31; late-night, 3, 26, 65, 67, 69, 78, 79, 80, 83, 110; political, 4; popularity of, 3, 5, 10, 16, 25, 42, 84, 85; reality shows and, 40, 47, 88, 95, 101, 115; "trash" talk shows, 87; variety shows and, 26, 69, 71,

90, 114. *See also Jan Publiek; Oprah Winfrey Show; Showto Na Slavi*
Tolson, Andrew, 4, 84
traditional values, 46, 47, 57, 58, 66, 83
trickster. *See* myth
Trifonov, Slavi, 16, 83, 110; actor, comic, 76; autobiography of, 68; cocreator of *Showto Na Slavi*, 18, 64; Cuckoo Band, performing with, 65; dynamism of, 69, 70, 73; entrance of, 71, 76; hyperbolic characters of, 71; interviewer, 80; *Showto Na Slavi*, host of, 67; MobilTel cell phone company, spokesperson for, 68; morphing character of, 68; *mutra* look of, 68; mythic dimensions of "Slavi," 5, 21, 67; popularity of, 69; prostitute in drag in *Cuckoo*, 64; protesting "Videnov's Winter," 64–65; village origins of, 68

Understanding Media, 8
United States, 2, 3, 6; afternoon talk shows in, 31, 37, 80; Bulgaria, impact on, 110; Bush, George W. (president of), 85, 97, 98–99; "class" television of, 112; colonialism of, 13; commercial television in, 30; "exceptionalism" of, 14; identity of "Americans" in, 13; *Jan Publiek*, influence on, 112; late-night talk shows in, 69; nationalism of, 12; race and racism in, 13; reception of television made in, 10; television programming of, 9; variety shows in, 69; wealth, relative, of, 11; women of, 90. *See also Oprah Winfrey Show*
utterance, 15, 23–24, 25, 46, 58, 59, 74, 113

Van Rompaey, Jan, 5, 16; aristocratic style of, 32; audience appreciation of, 30, 34; career of, 30, 35; coproducer of *Jan Publiek*, 31; democratic aims of, 31, 33; excellence of, 30–31; gender beliefs and behavior of, 31, 32; satirical style of, 21, 37, 41, 42, 45, 46; talents of, 30
VRT (Vlaamse Radio- en Televisieomroep), 29, 30, 31, 32, 35, 44

Walloonia. *See* Belgium
Winfrey, Oprah, 52, 86–90; artistic achievements of, 90; commercial stunts of, 106–7; ethos of, 104, 107; gender and, 102; oratorical prowess and performance of, 96–98, 101–2, 115. *See also* melodrama; *Oprah Winfrey Show*; rhetoric; television talk shows, afternoon
women: abused, 92; American, 90, 116; audience for the *Oprah Winfrey Show*, 89–90; class and, 50, 102, 115; democratic fantasy of, 88; elderly, 48, 50; equality and, 113; "family" rhetoric, of, 101, 107; female dancers on *Showto Na Slavi*, 71; feminine imaginary of, 89; feminism and, 86; flood victims, as, 104; gender and performance of, 39, 40, 47, 102 (*see also Jan Publiek*, panelists; Trifonov, Slavi; Van Rompaey, Jan; Winfrey, Oprah); girlfriends of *mutra*, 68; Islam and, 54, 58–61, 117; nurturing by, 116; panelists on *Jan Publiek* and, 31–32, 39; private sphere, in, 32; public sphere, in, 29, 39, 50, 100; self-help and 114

CPSIA information can be obtained at www.ICGtesting.com
Printed in the USA

236612LV00003B/10/P

07/11X